#DadLife

The Manly, Yet Reassuring,

I've-Got-This-Whole-Thing-Covered, *Relaxing,*

Therapeutic, Your-Kids-Are-Perfect-and-Fine,

Everything-Is-Perfect-and-Fine,

You'll-Never-Need-Another-Book, Book.

CHRIS BULTMAN

Contents

I'm a Dad

I'm a dad.

Just like you. Or maybe you're not a dad yet but you're about to be. Maybe you've just decided that you really want to be a dad—very soon or just someday soon. Maybe you've been a dad for a long time, and even have sons who are now fathers themselves.

No matter what, for whatever reason, you've found this book. And I'm honored. I hope you discover lessons that help you as much as they've helped me. My wish is that you find that you're not alone in your foibles and your fears. That you know you have support, and that you'll laugh, learn, feel connected, and remember the lessons and parenting practices that work for you.

They'll help other dads, too, you know, and what better gift can we give our children and fellow dads than our own stories and our own parenting practices.

I'm glad I'VE remembered the stories and lessons in my mind long enough that they came to the fruition and inspiration to have had that great light bulb tell me, YOU CAN TELL THESE STORIES.

I've never written a book before. I'm a visual creative. Perhaps in the recesses of my mind, like many of us, I've possibly pondered a book—a nebulous subconscious dream. This is another way I think you and I are alike.

There are so many stories to tell, and we all have important stories to tell. Each one different. So the desire to write a book? I'm pretty sure it lurked somewhere in the back of my mind as a fleeting consideration, a lark, something really cool to do.

I think, honestly, most of us, even if we don't consider ourselves writers, can picture ourselves writing a book. The Great American Novel is almost synonymous with the Great American dream in some ways, as stories have always led us to knowledge, to comfort, to lessons and to new convictions. In this book I have had the good fortune, and took the risk, to write these stories down.

And while this is no Great American Novel, it's my story. And I want to share it with you.

People have asked me how it came to be that I decided to write this book.

All I can say is that as you read on, you will learn that along with the idea and subsequent topic of every chapter, there is always a story behind it. And wherever there is a story, there is a lesson.

Those lessons turned into this first book. #DadLife

Maybe I wanted someone to talk to about this life as a dad. My children are the reasons—the how and the why—I learned these lessons myself. They're the reason I want to not only be a great dad, but to live it. They're the ones who made the stories, and the lessons.

They are why I've written this book.

They are, in the literal sense of the word, awesome. They inspire awe in me every day. And every day as a dad fills my minutes and hours with awe and wonder.

They make me want to be my best possible self, to live up to what they believe I am, to give them the answers and guidance they need to have a happy, purposeful life.

They are my LIFE. They're the reason I want to live a great Dad Life—a life worthy of them. I wouldn't have a Dad Life without them, obviously. But I've learned, thanks to these amazing children, that it's a major part of life I want—that of a father, a dad.

And they're amazing. They are miracles.

And so are yours. And because I think my children are awesome, and you think yours are awesome, too—there's a reason you've been drawn to this book. You're a dad, too.

Let me digress, or begin, with this story.

When you're a dad, there's always a story. Every day. And when you're a dad, all of it, every day, every lesson, every story, begins in a roundabout way.

You have to live it. Tell it. Then learn.

So there's this other thing—maybe it's how this whole thing began...

It Usually Starts Out Simple

I was sitting in my car, an "activity" that had become pretty much routine for me.

I wasn't in my car so much because I traveled frequently (sitting, you see, not driving). In fact, I didn't travel much at all. I have an office in my home and that's where I work. Let's just say that I don't visit the gas pump too frequently (something I'm rather happy about).

My car engine idled, emitting a low hum as I waited—five cars ahead of me and five cars behind me. I felt unsettled. Trapped. If I needed to, there'd be no way to escape. I couldn't wedge my way out of the car jam by going forward. There wasn't enough room. Changing my car gear to reverse would lead me to the same result. Nowhere.

And I was going to be there a while. About 45 minutes. I knew exactly how long this waiting was going to take. That hunk of metal didn't move when I did. At least not in this story. It couldn't always conform to my wishes. It usually had to conform to traffic.

My predicament?

The wait started at 2 p.m. The wait ended about 45 minutes later. The traffic? Well, usually a line-up of about 40 or 50 cars. Our engines humming even seemed to harmonize sometimes. Even though every car, or most cars, were rather different, the humming was the same. Almost like the purr of a cat? Or maybe a lion? Anyway, there were a lot of cars. A lot of people sitting in their driver's seats behind an idle engine. Usually, if you made a roll call, the same people, day after day, would say, "here." And what were we doing while sitting here? Well, all kinds of things. A lot of stuff. A lot of different things. We were all different sorts of people after all, with different temperaments and desires and timetables and interests.

Some drivers sat there patiently, almost as if they enjoyed the soothing hum of idling car engines and the time to be alone with their thoughts. Others cracked their windows and you could hear a steady beat, releasing the local radio station's latest hits into the air around them. Then you had those who saw this as an opportunity to assess the sometimes shameful but understandable state of their car's interior. The more frazzled picked up all the haphazard papers and receipts and fast food bags, stacking their trash in one easy spot to throw away as soon as they found a suitable receptacle. Others organized their center console, brushed the crumbs from their seats (we all had crumbs on our seats).

Then there was me. I liked to think of myself as a "hybrid driver," or "hybrid-person-sitting-behind-the-wheel-of-an-idling-car," if you want to be more specific. No, I didn't have a great energy-efficient vehicle. Actually, I didn't even attempt to make my car energy efficient at all. I never turned my car off to reduce the amount of carbon exhaust. It was almost always way too hot for that. I did live in Florida. Air-conditioning is the biggest selling point for every car in our state. Even clunkers MUST have AC. If you want to live or stay sane, your car HAS TO HAVE air-conditioning if you live in Florida. No, "hybrid driving" or "hybrid waiting" was more about my activities behind the wheel during those 45 minutes. Like a hybrid car, I was an energy-efficient human. I did a bunch of everything while I waited. I thought for awhile. I cleaned my car. I sat there in silence. I listened to the radio—loudly, quietly—that all depended on my mood (you'll find out about my moods later on in this book). I did it all.

This was a Monday through Friday ritual. At the same time. In the same place. And usually, this line of idled cars contained the same line-up of people.

What were we all doing? I mean, why? Why were we there every day, right on time, waiting, never missing a day? What was I doing?

I was waiting to pick up my children from school.

I work for myself, so I had the flexibility, even though I didn't necessarily have the time. But for my children, I made the time. I was committed to being present for my children. And part of that was accepting membership to this elite waiting-parent club, parents who picked up their children from school instead of leaving them to their own bus devices—I was going to be one of those dads who scooped up his kids fresh from school, ready to spend any time possible with them, especially RIGHT AS SCHOOL LET OUT.

They were in elementary school when I started. And even though they were young, they still carried a wide scope of emotions. Some days they showed an abundance of joy—because of their big accomplishments or exciting communions with new friends or the thrill of learning something they never knew before. Some days they were sad—because they didn't get to spend that extra five minutes on the playground at recess or didn't get the approval they sought from a favorite teacher. Other days, they were shy and somewhat aloof—because they didn't get the best conduct report for the day, and they didn't really want me to find out about that part (I always uncovered it, though. Maybe not immediately, but I was their dad. I found out everything. Eventually.).

Whatever their emotional state, I was happy to be present for it, to experience it first-hand. I didn't want to have to drag it out of them at dinner. Life was immediate for them, and by the time school had been over for just a little while, their experience and their emotions about it had almost all but dissolved. So to see their expressions and feel their energy and remember, in case I'd forgotten, the clothes they'd chosen to wear to school that day, meant everything to me. This was an important time. Not just in their day, but an important time in their lives.

And my life, too.

I wasn't there to pick them up and greet them at the end of every single one of their school days—but I was there for most of them. I tried to be. I made that effort to be.

So every day, one day after the other, with a line of cars and parents in front of me and behind me, I began to get less and less hybrid and started becoming one of those thinkers.

At first, my thinking was all about work—what needed to get done for clients, the meetings I needed to schedule, the perpetual, prodigal, endless to-do list. After awhile, my thoughts shifted to home life. Not necessarily about the children, but the things that needed to get done around the house.

Then something great happened. My mind seemed to tire of those thoughts and took a detour from the stuff that most dads focus on the most (the stuff that NEEDS TO GET DONE), to a less stressful, more pleasant train of thought—thoughts about my children.

I thought about who they were—as individuals and as MY CHILDREN. PART OF ME! I thought about their faces. Their personalities. Their attitudes. Their passions. Their charisma. Their favorite foods. Their favorite toys and books. The funny things they said. I thought about everything about them. Who they were right now. Children. And what life was like for them.

My daydream trajectory started going further.

I even started imagining their futures. How would their later years in elementary school go? Would they loathe or enjoy their transitions from elementary school to middle school, then middle school to high school.

And further.

What type of man would my daughter marry? How well would my son lead his family? I thought about them. All about them. Their present and their future and our time together.

As if I were in love. And of course I was.

Then I started focusing on my role in the lives of these amazing children I loved so much.

Dad. Leader. Provider. Teacher. It was up to me to keep them steady and sane. To teach them what they needed to know to not only get by in the world, but to succeed, to love themselves and their lives. It was all on me.

But I was up for the challenge. And I had the title to back it up.

I was DAD! *Their dad!*

Their life was important. Me being their dad was important. Both things together was a big deal!

Yes, I knew this, already—but the full force of the power of this very big deal hit me hard—the full weight, the full importance, the full miracle, the full opportunity. LIFE. I'd given them life, and together, we'd make it a great, powerful, thrilling adventure. The road would be hard sometimes, but we'd make it. I'd make it. The force of my love and of who I'd become—a father—had completely filled my spirit and I knew I could handle all of it.

So there I was. In an idle car, for at least 45 minutes a day for several days a week. Week after week. I waited for them and thought about them. And I made a choice. I wouldn't use this time to focus on any of those less-important aspects of my life. I wouldn't, as they say, lie on my death bed saying I wished I'd spent more time at the office or making sure my mortgage was always early or that my lawn was always perfect. I'd be thinking about my children. And my family. Nothing else.

They were one of the most important things that mattered. The job, the house—they were kept up and done well FOR THEM. My children were the stars in my life. Everything else was just the sky.

I like to know what to expect, as much as I can. I like to be as prepared as possible. I wanted an outline, a map; I wanted to know just what I should focus on to take advantage of my life, this Dad Life, that I was so excited to be a part of.

That dream and desire birthed this book #DadLife.

The # symbol is commonly used to incite response—call and response—a conversation on a specific topic. Hashtag, yes. It's a hashtag. But its purpose is a conversation topic. I wanted to talk about the life I was living. And a Dad Life was what I was living.

I want to have a conversation about dads.

I want to have a conversation with you. You, the soon to be dad. You, the dad with a two week old son or daughter. You, the dad who's had plenty of practice. And you, the dad who may even be a grandfather now, but who still needs to be the dad to your son as he travels the path of his own #DadLife.

Explore the lessons in this little tome I've written with love. Lessons I learned from my children and my own dad and his dad, too. Talk with your children about the lessons in this book—converse—it really needs to be a shared discussion. Not just your voice, but the voices of your children, too. Learn in the way that I learned, through trial and error and an open mind and especially, with unconditional love and a heart-deep desire to be the best father you can be. Seek. Seek to be your best dad-self as you travel this wonderful, once-in-a-lifetime, blessed journey—your own journey as a father, a dad, a person.

It's the most important part of your life—this being a dad, this chance to help mold very special people, your children, yourself, and in a wider sense, the world around you.

It's a new world. We want our children to see what their dad's Dad Life is like, and in the not too distant future, as you and your children grow, what this life of father and children was like for you, your children, all of us.

Dad Life isn't my journey; it's our journey. And Dad Life isn't my conversation topic; it's our topic.

So let's start talking.

CHAPTER 1

The One-Liner "Karate Chop"

I took my six year old son to a karate class once. We went to see if he had any interest and let him experience what happened in the class. But most importantly—it just sounded like a cool thing to do.

When the class started, the experienced students lined up. The instructor began the usual routine.

"Step into the ring. Kick your right leg high," he said. The children stepped into the ring and kicked their right legs as high as they could. "Keep right leg forward, planted firmly on the ground. Now. Swiftly cross both arms and chop your left then right hand through the air in a forceful motion."

My son, the class clown—a title that is both my bane and a source of great pride—performed his own interpretation of karate chops and kicks—all completely opposite of the instructor's command.

A loud voice instantly cut through the laughter. My son and I froze in a panic. The instructor's very serious admonishment stilled the room silent. From zero to 60, karate class flipped like a dime from a cool experience to an important skill complete with real-life application...and we didn't even know it was happening.

Within those first two minutes, we learned karate was about

discipline and not about performance.

The discipline guided the performance. The children knew what to do. Then they performed the action.

This knowledge—the awareness of what needed to be done before it could be done—was the key to their performance, the building block for every karate lesson to come.

And that was evident, quickly.

And then my brain kicked into daddy overdrive. Here's why:

We both came to this class without expectation. So my son responded in the best way he knew how. He likes to make people laugh. So he tried to be funny even in a serious environment. He didn't "misbehave." He simply didn't know better. Why? Because I hadn't taught him yet.

The Sensei established his authority. He laid out specific instructions. He carried out the plan. His students responded with respect and positivity. And they followed his instructions.

I hadn't done that with my son. Yet.

And even though I entered the class with innocence, I left with self-knowledge—and an action plan.

When a Sensei gives a single-lined command, his students follow it almost like a reflex.

In day-to-day life, a Sensei-style one-liner offers dads the perfect way to sum up what they expect from their children.

This one-liner arms children with the tools they need to be well-behaved in any situation, thus providing a crystal clear understanding of how to act, react, and communicate effectively and appropriately.

Because of this karate class experience, I call my one-liner the "Karate Chop."

It packs some punch, hits hard, and, if the child doesn't follow through, involves real-life consequences. When children do follow through, the result itself packs a sweet, powerful and lasting punch for everyone—and the positive experience encourages children to follow through again and again.

The "Karate Chop" wraps up all your expectations into a powerful, quick-witted phrase you can use repeatedly, integrate anywhere, and remember forever.

Make your one-liner clear and concise enough that children of any age can understand it. Make it direct so children can learn how important it is. And perhaps the biggest rule of all, be sure it's something that won't have to change as the children get older.

That's Why the "Karate Chop" Works So Well

See, the action of a karate chop is impactful, and the discipline behind it not only builds character but lasts a long time, too. It's not malicious or shaming. It creates a simple, powerful lesson.

Period.

My personal "karate chop" requests four things of my children, and they're simple:

Be kind, respectful, obedient…and (as my son taught me) HAVE FUN!

My Personal One-Liner Policies

Be Kind

Kindness brings about better relationships, fuller lives, and a positive effect on the people and world around you. Kind people have a leg up in the world. Isn't that what we want for our children anyway?

Be Respectful

Respect is simple. It's showing—through action, through listening, and through speaking—that someone else, besides yourself, is important. You minimize conflict, build stronger relationships, and help others feel good about themselves.

Be Obedient

Obedience builds character. Character builds a solid foundation from which to grow a good life. It is that simple and that important.

Have Fun

Having fun is crucial here, however, because if your children feel like they are having fun, they are more apt to buy into the other rules you set for them. Master the art of the buy-in, and once you have it from your kids, they learn to master the art of the "karate chop," too.

Integrate the "Karate Chop" Into Everyday Life

Here's where you need patience—and lots of it. Practice is paramount. You cannot perfect this system in an instant. It takes time for you to demonstrate technique and for the children to understand the form. Again, this takes practice—lots and lots of practice. Did I mention practice?

How to Create Your Own One-Liner

Introduce the Concept

Why are you teaching your kids the karate chop? If you don't know why you're teaching them and don't believe it will work, why would they do it? Why would they believe it? Answer? They won't believe it and they won't do it.

Develop Your Own One-Liner

Create a simple "karate chop" one-liner of your own. One that makes sense to you. Ensure it covers a strong, easy-to-understand concept and clear set of expectations.

The key here is to make it simple, simple, simple.

Karate chops happen with a quickness. Your one-liner should be just as quick while packing a major punch in the learning department.

Teach Your Children the Consequences of Your Karate Chop

Every action your child makes begets a consequence. Consequences can be positive. They can be negative, too. Always point out the positive aspect of a consequence first, no matter how small it may appear to be and even if the consequence itself will eventually be negative.

Why? Children (and, let's face it, grown-ups, too) react better and learn more from positive reinforcement and constructive criticism—which begins with positivity and understanding even if it is followed by disciplinary action.

Positivity helps us feel good about ourselves. It helps us feel safe and loved. It encourages us to do better. And if your children decide not to abide by the karate chop, a negative and disciplinary consequence should follow, but not without love.

Always meet your children where they are. And always cast everything you do for and say to your children in the light of positivity. Let that light surround and lead the way in all parts of your relationship with your children. Even and especially when it comes to discipline.

(And no, I DO NOT recommend a real life karate chop on your child. If that's what you do, there are other books to help you with that issue.)

Look At It This Way

Karate students, at some point during their lessons, must chop a wooden board—clean through, with a single chop—to move up to a higher belt. Their technique incorporates the Sensei's training of learned expectations, positive reinforcement and the experience of both good and bad consequences. If the karate chop is performed properly, the board will break—sans any negative consequences.

But if the chopper loses focus, breaks form, and falls out of rhythm, his karate chop does not break the board at all. And all the child is left with is a hurt hand, and probably some hurt pride, too.

Likewise, if your children do not follow the one-liner you've laid out for them, they won't break their board either.

Identify the Reward

Every child in every family has their own idea of "reward." For some, it's extra playtime with friends. For others, a reprieve from one day of chores fits the bill. For my children, if they get to stay up a little past their regular bedtime, they feel like they've struck gold!

So choose a reward that excites them.

Let's Pause for a Second

Of course, tangible rewards don't provide lasting success. But when we show them that we are proud of them—in an immediate way they can understand—it demonstrates how much we love them.

And even when they don't succeed and while they may not receive a tangible reward, when we show them that we love them unconditionally no matter what, that is the ultimate reward—for our kids, and for ourselves, too.

Start Practicing the "Karate Chop"

What time is the right time to incorporate the "karate chop?" I use my "karate chop" at almost every given opportunity, especially when the propensity for not following it is at its greatest.

For instance, right before a long car ride or when their friends are around. Before these festivities begin, I remind my children about the "karate chop."

Use your own one-liner at expected times in the daily schedule—when they'll have the greatest impact. This helps ingrain its implication into their minds, especially when they're about to start something big.

Remind Your Children About the "Karate Chop"

The best time to make these reminders are for the times you'll be using it most.

For instance, every time we settle into the car for a trip, I ask my children to explain the meaning of the "karate chop."

I even turn it into a game to find out who can give me the fastest, most accurate answer. (My children respond twice as fast when it's a game.)

Don't Forget to Have Fun

Remember when I mentioned that your "karate chop" should be fun? This is important. Fun influences success big time. Children are all for fun. Don't bore them with serious lectures. Your words will go into one ear and out of the other as soon as you begin talking. So have fun.

Communicate your message. Reinforce how serious it is. But make it fun.

Use a silly voice. Give high fives. Celebrate at high volume when they've gotten the answers right. You know your children. They make you feel like a kid yourself—if you let them. Be creative. Your children will show you the way, I promise.

Lastly, Strive for Improvement, Not Perfection

Don't give up. This is vital. Your "karate chop" may seem for naught. But if you continue to implement it regardless of positive or negative results, you'll eventually get—albeit not that often at first—positive responses.

Whether or not they succeed, keep doing it. Practice. Practice it over and over and over. Quite often, children choose to ignore what they've learned. Why? The answer's simple. They're children. Children just don't do everything you've asked of them every minute of every day. Whether or not they succeed, keep doing it. Practice. Practice it over and over and over.

No matter what their reaction, remember that you are building the foundation for their decision-making and it will stick. Keep using your one-liner consistently. Every time a situation arises, use the one-liner, and they will soon learn to identify the response you've established with them.

(Notice I said "with them." At this point, the buy-in has already happened and the "karate chop" is theirs just as much as it is yours.)

The results take time. A lot of time. But the effort is worth it.

Rinse and Repeat

After you create your "karate chop," integrate it into your daily life with your kids and never stop practicing it.

And don't forget to repeat, repeat, repeat. You may get sick of hearing your own voice. But keep the repetition going. Results vary—because all children are different. It may not always be perfect (and nothing is ever perfect), but stick it out and the results will get stronger and stronger.

But Trust Me, this Works!

My children understand the purpose of our "karate chop." When I took my son to that fateful karate class, we had no "karate chop" method in place. Then inspiration set in and my "karate chop" one-liner entered the light, changing things dramatically and making our lives easier.

I started working on the one-liner with my children. They showed no interest. Over time, however, they started learning its value. I got their "buy-in." On a recent trip, before we headed out, I forgot to review our "karate chop" plan of action.

My children said, "Dad, aren't you forgetting something?" Now, while it's definitely not perfection all the time, dads, that is definitely progress!

Hiyah!

(Now. Go ahead and create your own "karate chop!")

What My Son Said

My son: "Dad, we need a parrot. That way, if I do anything wrong, I can just blame it on him."

Age: 7

CHAPTER 2

The Memory Bank

It was morning. The house stood still. Well, it always stood still, but I'm talking about palpable, literal quiet, which isn't normal in my house. C'mon, I have young children. They are hyper. That massive amount of energy translates to noise. Running. Screaming. Even their "inside voices" are the kinds of piercing decibels non-parents might call noise pollution. But hey, they're children. You know how it is. Right, dads?

So just imagine me laying there in bed, barely awake and in full realization that I had a quiet house. Peaceful. This joyous moment was one to celebrate. The celebration? A trip back to la-la land with my face buried deep into my fluffy pillow as I (for once) focused on "ZZZs" instead of "A-B-C's.

It didn't happen often. But you BETTER BELIEVE I was about to take full advantage of this moment. After all, it could be an anomaly and I may never experience this. Like ever. Again.

So there I was, warm in my bed half-awake-half-asleep in absolute bliss about the wonderful knowledge that I was about to get sooo much extra sleep.

And *juuuust* as my eyes were beginning to close and my consciousness faded toward the final destination of luxuriously deep sleep I wouldn't want to wake from, it hit me.

MY CHILDREN AREN'T MAKING ANY NOISE!

Not a peep. Nothing. Nada. I mean, my house was quiet. QUIET. My house is never quiet. Never. Ever. Heck, even when the children are at their best, there is a buzz happening in this place. My house. My casa. A place of relaxation. You know, the kind where you can sit back and fall asleep with the best white noise possible—children having the time of their lives (yes, I'd like to think they enjoy this place).

I sprung straight up to my feet in an instant. It was weird. A split second earlier, I was face down and drifting into an abyss of dreamland utopia. Now I was standing up, adrenaline pumping, my attention on full alert, and ready to leave my bedroom in a hurry. I transformed from that lazy I-wish-I-were-sleeping-still dad to a fierce, Rambo-like man ready to kill to protect those that I loved. After all, I didn't know what was going on. I had to be ready for anything. Hence, the Rambo imitation.

Where were my children? What were they doing? Why didn't I hear them? Why was this house *soooooo* quiet?

I left my bedroom determined to find answers. I was calm but I was ready for action. (Ok, so I said I was Rambo. So, maybe I wasn't *that* calm). What if something happened? I didn't have time for questions, only answers. I left my bedroom determined to get them.

I searched room to room. I was quiet. I didn't know what I would find. Or if I would find anything at all. I was in that stealth daddy mode. It was kind of cool. But I didn't have time to think of how awesome I was in my approach. I had children to find.

And of course (it always happens this way, in the very last place, I checked, I spotted them.)

In the living room.

With their their backs to me, faces reflected in the computer monitor screens, eyes gleaming with excitement. They *knew* they weren't allowed on the computer—*my* computer. Dad's computer. It was an important toy of mine (plus, my work computer). They knew this was off limits.

But there they were, my daughter stood next to the computer, with a posture communicating that she was well aware that what they were doing was wrong and her stance said, "I'm ready for a quick getaway *right now.*" My son on the other hand, well, he sat atop the desk clad in only his underwear. *Reclining* with a posture that said, "I belong here. This place is mine. I'm not going *anywhere.*" Even their body language reflected their endearingly contrasting personalities. It was pretty funny for sure.

They were still oblivious of my stealth-ninja-dad presence, so I stood there, just watching. I wasn't thinking of a harsh correction (you'll learn later in this book that I dish out "corrections" rather than "punishments"). I enjoyed listening to the soft whispers between them as they worked through their attempts to navigate the machine.

Oh, they thought they had me!

My first reaction? It may be a little different than some would expect. This was MY machine. My computer. My baby. Some men fall in love with cars, but not me. I was in love with my computer. And even though I treasured this machine, my reaction matched with something I love to do.

I laughed.

Then I grabbed my smartphone and started recording. After a few seconds of recording them, I yelled, "HEY!"

In the swift moment of worry that followed, they turned around in terror. They were busted! They knew they were busted. My son leaped off the desk with a quickness and my daughter sprang for the hills. But of course I wouldn't let her. My arm reached out to a length that felt like an eternity to guide my sweet little daughter right in front of me once again. And even before this, their eyes grew larger than my worry, forcing my mouth to crack a smile.

"Stay right there!", I said to them, trying to cover up that smirk trying desperately to show itself. Once their nerves settled, they noticed I had the camera on them, documenting the whole incident.

Then my four-year-old son said it, "Don't post this on Facebook!!"

I didn't post it on Facebook, or anywhere. But it was something

I wanted to see again. And I wanted my children to see it again.

When I was growing up—whether it was at family events or in the privacy of our home, I performed all sorts of funny antics to entertain my brothers and sisters—all in an attempt to steal my parents' attention. Because I was so entertaining and funny— the outgoing jokester that I was—it worked most of the time. And when it didn't work, I didn't stop until it did.

I remember one inevitable result that happened no matter what. My parents documented them—as well as they could, anyway, given the more limited technology of the time. This limited technology I speak of? I'm sure you remember it quite fondly yourself. Well, I was an 80's baby. That meant that I often saw my dad lugging around a huge black hunk of plastic. It routinely sat squarely on his shoulder and his hand went through a tight strap that wrapped around his hand. A red light flashed signifying we were "live!" We were young at the time and never heard the phrase "Lights. Camera. Action!" But we sure did know what it meant. We were in prime time. The audience? Well, we didn't care. We just knew that my dad had his VHS style video recorder. It was large, but our stardom always superseded it!

Recently, when visiting my parents' house, I asked about those recorded memories. Before I knew it, I had an old plastic bin filled with old pictures of me and my siblings doing just about everything. I was glued to that box for hours.

I couldn't believe the memories that I helped make. I couldn't believe there were moments that escaped my memory. My parents remembered all of them, mainly because they had physical evidence.

I want to document the life of my children to an even better degree than what my parents were able to do. For after all, each note and image sparked a fond childhood memory—one that may not have been remembered were it not for my parents who captured them. Plus, my children are awesome. They are funny. They do the coolest things ever. At least to me. I'm sure yours are the same for you. Either way, these days, we have many more ways to keep precious memories preserved forever, like those secret government files no one can unlock—but I want them seen, I just want them safe. And I plan on using our technology to my advantage. You should too.

Today, our children live in a fast-paced world filled with enough ever-evolving technology to document almost anything you can imagine—with easy-access tools that let us make memories by simply pulling our phones from our pockets.

I urge you to use these tools.

Everyone chooses to document differently and some more than others. I tend to document more than the average person, but that's because I find every second—big or small—a precious memory.

Before I go any further, I need to mention something.

You're always going to have someone comment on your level of documentation. Even if the recordings and pics are of your beautiful children—some people find it too invasive. Others find it endearing. So just document at your own personal comfort level.

At the end of your life—and even as your children grow—these images and videos make up your family's box of priceless treasures, your own personal testament to a life well-lived, one filled with the greatness of childhood and your own personal joys.

This is something no one can take away from you.

Documentation. Let's Cover That

Milestones

Milestones are the most important things to document, because your children achieve their kindergarten diploma only once. They learn to ride their bike for the first time only once. They're not going to hit that same milestone again. Ever. There is only one "once."

When my son was six, he learned how to ride his bike. He asked that I come outside. He was confident and told me I would be seeing him ride his bike. I was slightly hesitant. He knew it was time. Me, on the other hand, well, I wasn't so sure considering we didn't practice as much as I thought we should.

"I've got this dad", he said. My son was confident. He had swagger. He said this with a cool red helmet and a white tank top on, almost as if he would add gold chains around his neck if I let him. In other words, the swagger in his words matched his appearance. He was a cool kid. And, he was positive he would do anything he claimed he would. And to my surprise (seriously,

I was pretty surprised), that boy got on his bike and peddled his little heart out. Before I could tell him "good job!", he was already two houses away.

Milestones. They come and go quickly. You better document these!

Funny Moments

As the old adage goes, kids say (and do) the darndest things. And these darndest things are often hilarious. For instance, my son happens to be a master at uttering the funniest and most random statements. And I've been capturing them for years.

But, anyone can say that their children are funny. But, because I've been documenting these funny moments for years now, I've got the proof. Here is a conversation my son had with me. It was serious. Seriously, funny. Oh yea, he was 7 at the time.

> **My Son:** "Dad, can two of my friends come in to play?"
> **Me:** "Well, what are you going to do?"
> **My Son:** "We are going to wrestle!"
> **Me:** "Uhhhh....."
> **My Son:** "Don't worry dad, I've made an 8 year old boy cry like a little girl before!"

Some people tell tall tales of their funny children, but I just show them these quotes. When you document your children, you can do the same.

Funny Moments. They are funny when they happen and they're even funnier when you relive them. Yea, you better document these!

Growth

Physical growth charts are nothing new. But they're worth looking at as your children get older—and bigger. They'll never be this size again. So with a growth chart, why not try and resist marking up the nearest wall to record their ever-evolving heights?

If and when your family moves, you can't take that wall with you. Instead, use a portable, light piece of narrow wood so you can keep the memory with you as you travel through life. Young children grow fast, so measure their new stature at least once every six months. As they get older, once a year will work just fine.

Growing up, my mom always asked if she needed to "put a brick on my head to slow me down." I inadvertently use the same phrase with my son. I heard this often as I grew. And, I grew often. Even though we moved several times growing up, we had a long thin piece of wood that my dad kept in the garage with markings of our growth.

Each time he pulled it out, we relived each year and every tick mark. The higher those tick marks got the more memories we had to talk about. And since I grew a lot, there was always a lot to talk about. Plus, I loved having bragging rights over my brother that I was taller than him at certain ages. Unfortunately, he won out and is an inch taller than me to this day.

Growth. You may document an inch, but your memories will go on forever. Don't forget to add your tick marks!

Letters

Of course, you're mainly the collector of this documentation as these are created by your kids. You just happen to be the repository and it's your job to keep them in a safe place. As your children begin to write and write you letters—store them. These letters are a definite treasure, words you'll want to revisit. And since kids are so often just naturally and unwittingly funny, reading them again will certainly gift you with quite a few laughs.

Recently, I visited some of my extended family for Thanksgiving. My aunt, one who was labeled the "cool aunt" growing up, mainly because she would spoil us with every type of sports gear known to man because she worked in the corporate world at one of the major sports retailers out there.

She pulled me aside and handed me a framed letter. This letter. It made me chuckle. It was addressed to her. The writer, well, that would be me. It's contents said:

Thank you for the shoes! They make me run so fast!!!

Love, Christopher

I wrote this? I didn't even remember this. But as I read it a second time, I painted a picture of me as a little boy lined up in a race. Before the shotgun kicked off the start of it, I glanced down and saw my shiny blue (it was my favorite color growing up) shoes. When the race started, clearly I won. Because of the shoes, of course. This simple note sparked my imagination. This memory was worth revisiting.

I thanked her for sharing this with me. It made me think of myself as a child. It was a good memory (even if I did had to fill in the missing pieces).

Letters. They are words on a page that will create a memory for a lifetime. Store them, they are invaluable!

Events

Of course, throughout their growing-up years, your children are likely to be involved in all sorts of events. A school play where lines are forgotten. A family reunion where your kids don't remember a single distant relative. A visit to the dentist's office that they would actually hope to forget. Any event is noteworthy.

One of the first noteable events (for a dad), that I remember documenting of my son was his first basketball game. The little boys on the team were three and four years old. My son, just turned 4. Watching the game provided more hilarity than suspense. The basketball court looked like a busy bee hive with worker bees flying around unsure of their destination.

My son loved to run. I don't think he really knew what he was running to. Or what he was running for. But, seriously, this didn't matter. The coaches assisted as best as they could. And one assist proved to be worth documenting.

One coach grabbed the ball and put it into my sons hands. They yelled "Go down and shoot the ball." My son was a machine! He took the ball in hand, ran like a linebacker weaving in and out of little boys who were running in circles as he headed near the basket. He didn't dribble the ball at all. Not even once. He held it strong and was determined to score (even though he didn't understand the meaning behind it).

A foot away from the goal, he kneeled down and heaved his body - and the ball - upward, toward the rim. The ball was hurled into the air. It was spinning counterclockwise ferociously as I started to leave my seat cheering him on. Imagine a slow-motion film where one dad is cheering louder than all the other parents in the gym. That was me. Picture a spinning basketball nearing the tip of the rim as my eyes grew larger while his arms were simultaneously clapping, yet holding a jittery camera, all while his arms were going straight up into the air. Yes, that was me too. The ball started its downward motion as gravity quickly (yet, oh so slowly) took over. The ball (still spinning) passed the edge of the basketball rim and did a "swish" as the net swayed back and forth from the ball passing through it.

My son scored his FIRST EVER basket! And, I had it all on video!

Events. Because you're caught up in the moment, documenting them gives you a different look at it later. They are worth taking note!

How Should You Best Capture Your Memories?

While capturing options are practically endless, let me narrow the list down to our era's top and most important means with which to keep a record of your kids—at least as far as I'm concerned.

Facebook

As I write this book, over ONE BILLION PEOPLE are signed up on Facebook. That's right, I said one BILLION! In other words, this social connection platform is not going away anytime soon. Use Facebook for day-to-day posts and pictures—and be sure to tag them so you can easily find these old posts later. Right now, Facebook is currently formatted to act as a "living timeline." And hey, that's pretty cool considering we are talking about capturing your children's own living timeline.

What do I (Personally) Capture on Facebook?

#DadLife Quotes

I like to engage the people I know with general thoughts on living the dad life. Call it encouragement, if you will. I tag each one of these with the hashtag #DadLife. A quick example:

> *Don't expect your children to do their chores when the rest of the house isn't in order. As a parent, your example is much stronger than your words.*

> *#DadLife*

Quotes from My Children

My friends and family visit my Facebook page often to find out, literally, what my children are saying. Right now, these quotes are more often centered upon my son because he says randomly funny things all the time. I tag each of these posts with the hashtag #WhatMySonSaid. My daughter also has her fair share of great quotes. I tag those with the hashtag #WhatMyDaughterSaid. You can easily filter these to see all your quotes in one location. Here's a good one:

> **My Son:** *"I hurt my head and need an ice pack."*
> **Me:** *"Ok, go get one..."*
> **My Son:** *"Ok, I got one..."*
> **Me:** *"Go put that back, that's a popsicle."*
> **My Son:** *"Why?"*
> **Me:** *"Because if it melts, it'll get everywhere."*
> **My Son:** *"Don't worry dad, I'll eat it by then."*

> *#WhatMySonSaid*

Pictures

Any time we're up to something special, I capture it with a picture, post it on Facebook, tag our current location, and write a brief description of it. This gives me a real-time update on our happenings and just how we were feeling at that very moment.

Important Notes
Lots of people feel like their information is unsafe when they post it to Facebook, especially when it comes to their children. Be sure to learn about your page's privacy settings.

Also, Facebook offers a "download" button that allows you to store all of your online Facebook posts to your own computer. So, there is no need to post on Facebook and document separately.

Physical Paper

No matter how "digital" you think you are, there are just some things that can't be documented that way. For instance, real live paper you can touch! Your children create these wonderful mementos at school and home—on actual, tangible, good old-fashioned paper—and they delight in sharing these creations with you. Whether it's a surprise letter or picture or a school art project or essay, I recommend two ways to properly store these treasures.

Filing Cabinet

Take a note from your parents' generation and store important keepsakes the good ole' fashioned way—in a filing cabinet or a box. Sort them by child and even by year if you would like to store a lot.

Digital Storage

Bring in some of today's new technology to help with long-term clutter. If you aren't an organized person, this is especially helpful. I often pull out my smartphone and snap a picture of that work of art my children bring to me. (I even post it directly to Facebook).

See, the best of both worlds.

Get creative. Discover the capturing methods that works best for you. I've simply suggested what works best for me. And, if you can't remember some of my suggestions, don't forget to document your notes to remember!

Capturing. How Much is Too Much?

Your volume of capturing really depends upon your own personal preferences and personality. In my experience, this boils down to a few types of dad documentarians:

The Hyper-Detailed Dad

He captures everything—and I mean everything. For instance, his child just finished drinking a glass of water. Yep, he documented it. He has the ability to look at a date and specific time and pretty much know exactly what his children were doing. These types of dads generally have plenty of time to revisit their past more often. So in theory, this minutiae of memories is excellent for them.

The Committed and Consistent Dad

He captures the memorable life experiences of his children—the major milestones, the funny moments and the significant events. All on a regular basis. He may overlook some of the smaller acts in life but you better believe that he is lined up in the first row watching you swing a bat at your baseball game. Remember, he is committed. So, you never have to look over your shoulder in the stands to know if he is there. Because, he is. And, with his camera.

The Casual Dad

He captures when he has time rather than forcing himself to have time. When you do this, however, you often write down notes of a memory long after it happens instead of capturing the actual moment—and then sometimes forget to even write down that important memory altogether. So, details are accounted for but can sometimes be blurry at best. But, a blurry detail is always better than no detail. So, the casual dad still has its perks. Any documenting dad is a great dad no matter what.

Decide which category you fit in and own it. Again, don't worry about the dad documentarians around you. Document based on your comfort level and style—not someone else's.

But, Really. Why Capture?

A lot of people assume that you are documenting everything about your children just for yourself. Nope. Not even close. Remember, you may have extended family who don't live nearby but would still love to give your children a long-reached pinch on the cheek if they could. And they will, if you give them that picture, no matter how far away you're calling from.

Friends and family alike love keeping up-to-date on your super-cool family's latest happenings. You're doing this for the kids, too, of course. One day, sooner than you think, your children will be at an age where it's important to them to see who they were, what they have done and how they have changed over the years.

My son is aware of my documenting. Even though he was six years old, he told me he wanted to talk to me about my Facebook information that I was sharing. He asked me after a very specific post.

We were outside of my parents house—a particularly favorite playspot in my parents' backyard. He played for a while, and naturally, he got tired, then he got a little irritable. (But not nearly as much as some of the irritability that I display at times. Keep reading in this book, I give you a sneak peek later on. Promise.). His behavior led to a quick timeout on the sidewalk.

His body language showed him pouting. He was sitting down, knees up with his face buried in his hands, looking toward the ground.

I couldn't help myself. While I clearly did not feel his behavior was the best, I wanted to capture his stance to show him later. MUCH later in life. It was something I thought would be funny later, when he grew up. I did what I normally did when I thought something was funny.

I posted it on Facebook.

After he got up, he heard me talking with my sister about my post to Facebook. With a tear trickling down his eye, he asked why I shared that with everyone.

I didn't think about how it would impact him.

Now, my son and I keep an open dialogue about what I share. I share his funny thoughts all the time but if I feel it's too personal, him and I discuss it. Even though he's young, he knows he has the freedom and respect to have an intelligent conversation with me about it.

So remember, life happens fast and it only happens once. How you decide to use that time and capture your memories is important. No matter how you practice your dad-documentarian style, just make it count.

Be a dad who documents!

What My Son Said

Me: "What are we going to do?"

My son: "Let's think about the logical thing to do. I mean, do dogs chase their own tail?"

Age: 6

CHAPTER 3

Let Logic Rule (Your Discipline)

I remember when my children were infants. Holding them in my arms, feeding them in their high chairs, playing with them as they crawled around on the floor. They expressed themselves with funny little sounds—little chirps, long "aaaaaahs," nonsensical "bahs" and sweet funny "dah, dah, dahs," that were almost conversational. Just like every other parent with a baby, I responded with funny noises myself, spoke to them just like they did, in a foreign language that made sense only to us. My goal was to get that sweet smile on their faces, those heart-warming laughs. And for what I was trying to accomplish, it worked.

As they started to get older, I questioned whether or not I should follow the "typical" parental path in communicating with my child, whatever that was. What worked? What didn't work? What was the best way to handle tough situations? What were things I should steer clear from?

I wanted to be a great dad, and I wrestled all the time with what that entailed, for with each passing day as a parent, I could never redo my actions and reactions again. Every moment mattered. Every action counted. This was important stuff and I did not want to screw it up.

So I began incorporating logic—a step-by-step analysis wherein I played out every imaginable scenario and what the logical conclusion, reaction and action would be.

Then it came to me as suddenly as your brand-new child actually appears in the delivery room: why not introduce the same logic I'd been using in my head and apply it directly to how I interacted with my children?

Logic is simple in theory, but it can take some work to grasp in practical applications. So it's important to stick with it. And you can expect to slip up, too. But no matter what you face in life, you have a choice of how to respond and behave, and so do your children. Their choices are the responses they decide to make. Most people decide to respond in one of two crucial ways:

Emotionally or Logically

Emotional responses are practically knee-jerk reactions that happen quickly and unpredictably. They can be positive or negative. The results can be perfect or catastrophic. But these reactions are almost always extreme and erratic. There's no consistency.

Logical responses are patient and thoughtful. They come with a pause and are designed to be thought-provoking and to spark the logical side of the brain, which is calm and consistent. Logic leaves emotion at the door and does not make room for scattered, unpredictable, emotion-filled responses. With logic, you weigh the options and devise the best course of action.

There's nothing wrong with being emotional, of course. We want to teach our children to share their emotions. We want them to be sensitive and loving and empathetic and joyful and

expressive. However, for the sake of this chapter's lessons on logical discipline, the word "emotional" means "too quick to respond because I didn't think things through properly."
Are you following me? Excellent!

I did not want to be an emotional dad. I also did not want to raise my children to make emotional decisions, but I did want them to always be mindful of their emotions. I set out to provide the security, stability, and consistency they would need in an erratic, unpredictable world that can foster emotional instability and uncertainty—in children and in adults. But the sooner you make your big decisions based on logic rather than emotion, the better able you'll be to face the curveballs life is bound to throw your way.

You can introduce logic to your children in all sorts of ways. To keep it simple, I'll focus on the most important area I feel that logic should be presented, integrated, and carried out.

Logic Through Discipline

No matter how great the parent and how spectacular the child, there will be a time where discipline needs to be considered. While thousands of books have been written on every type of child discipline, I will focus on one: my own, and how I arrived there. I think you're going to love this.

Implement Correction, Not Punishment

My grandfather, one of the wisest men I know, taught me that we should teach our children to correct their behavior rather than punish them for it. A correction warrants a shift in attitude whereas a punishment instills a judgment that you are bad simply for something you have done. One thrives to teach a change and the other focuses on your bad behavior alone. And it works. In my home, we now have "corrections" instead of "punishments." My children understand the difference and they accept corrections much better.

Talk Before Acting

It's important to always give your children the opportunity to explain themselves. What may seem like one thing could be something completely different. I admit, I've jumped to plenty of conclusions with my children. Conclusions solve nothing. It only heightens your emotions. Remain calm and let your child lead the conversation. "Tell me what happened," is a simple enough lead-in for them to take over. (Yes, I said, "take over." It's OK to give your child a platform to lead the conversation even during discipline.) Remember, a parent who is integrating logic through discipline cannot act emotionally by showing frustration or anger. Your calm demeanor is important to reinforcing the logic. (Don't worry, you will still act emotional at times. I do. And that's alright. No one is perfect!)

Integrate the Logic

If you have identified an action you find to be wrong, hold off on the punishment (ahem…I mean the "correction") part. First, walk your children through the logical steps that help them discover why their action was wrong. Ask your children a series of simple questions immediately after you see them behave in a way you find unacceptable.

(It is best to do this in a quiet setting with just yourself, your child, and no external distractions. When I take this approach, my son pays complete attention to what needs to be communicated... Otherwise, in public, the best word to describe the resulting scene would be, let's just say, unpredictable...)

The following questions begin with the need for a simple response and logically leads your children to a more detailed and revealing response. This also helps with better communication between you and your child while giving you more information.

Ok, lets try it.

Start by asking these questions, in order, to your children:

- Did you know what you did was wrong? (Allow a yes or no response)
- How did you know it was wrong? (Allow a full response)
- Did you think anything would happen if your were caught? (Yes or no)
- What do you think the consequences are for your actions? (Full response)
- Why do you think you deserve the consequence? (Full response)
- Did I choose to give you this consequence? (Yes or no)
- Who chose the consequence? (Full response)

Dads, do you see the logical progression in these questions? You are trying to guide them down the logical path where the ending point results in a decision they've made instead of a consequence you chose to give them.

They chose to do something wrong. They know there is a consequence. They chose to receive the consequence. None of this is something you chose for them. As a parent, you would choose for them to always have fun and never be in trouble.

All good in theory though, right?

Let's Get Real. A Very Real Life Example

Each day, my son comes home from the second grade with a class folder he's supposed to show me. This folder gives me a view of his classroom life. It includes his work, his classroom news, tests, drawings, and just about everything a parent wants to know about how their child's day goes at school. You name it, if he's done it, it's in there. (Well, most of the time.)

This folder's purpose? A direct communication from school to home. It's meant for me to look at everyday so I know what's going on.

One particular day, I asked to see the folder. I opened it up and looked in the left hand pocket—the one labeled "keep at home." This typically included homework assignments and tests that his teacher has already graded and recorded.

Scanning through his graded tests—ones I'd already signed and sent back to school—I noticed something was off. There was no light bulb of recognition about what I was looking at. Instead, it was more like I was scratching the side of my head in confusion.

With each paper I went through, I became more confused.

Why could I not remember any of these tests?

I signed them. I turned them back in. The teacher saw that I saw them and put them in the "keep at home" pocket which meant that we were good to go.

But we were *not* good to go.

I quickly looked for my signature and found each of them positioned in the middle of the pages. They were a bit lighter than normal. And, they clearly were about six inches higher on the page than I normally signed the sheets. And then it hit me!

My son forged my signature.

I didn't want to jump to conclusions. Maybe he didn't. Hmmm. I was confused. I wasn't sure if he did or not. He was in second grade. I didn't know this craft at that age. This skill of deception. There was no way he could know this high-level of duplicity yet, right? Nonetheless, I had to get to the bottom of this.

"Did you sign my name on your papers?" I asked in an admittedly assumptive voice. See, I don't ever want to "assume" anything when it comes to my children. But there was one thing I knew. I didn't sign these papers. I assumed anyway. My son had to be the culprit. He just needed to admit it.

He didn't answer me. He just gazed at me deeply, almost as if he were hypnotizing me into believing someone else was the culprit. He was trying to thwart me, but this time I wasn't going to fall for it.

I told him to go to his room. I needed a moment to process this. He was guilty. He all but admitted he was guilty. I was upset. A part of me was also impressed. I wasn't impressed with his actions, just that he had the smarts enough to come up with such a mastermind plan to sidestep this precarious and dangerous dilemma. But did he really have a dilemma? I was completely confused because I didn't think someone his age was even capable of doing something like this. Where would he learn how to do something like this? Definitely not from me.

He was going to be in so much trouble!

After 15 minutes of thinking and thinking and thinking of my next move, I went into my son's room and found him sitting on his bed. He wasn't smiling. He also wasn't crying. He looked dumbfounded. Perhaps he was questioning how obvious his trick had been. Maybe he was realizing my "dad knows everything" comments I have on repeat may actually be true (this time).

I went straight into interrogation mode—my first line of defense. Remember those questions we just went over? Yeah, these have officially kicked into this story.

"Did you know what you did was wrong?" I asked him while standing and waiting for a response.

He looked at me with those puppy dog eyes that included a classic tear rolling down his cheek. He didn't mutter a response. He simply nodded his head in the form of a "yes," signifying an agreement.

I followed by asking, "How did you know it was wrong?" I wasn't going to accept a one word answer. I wanted an explanation. And I was certain I was going to get it. A response was needed here. First, I needed a better understanding. I needed to hear out loud why he did what he did. After all, he may not have given his actions much thought until now. He needed to hear his answer as well.

It didn't come quick. I stood patiently waiting for one. He knew that I wasn't going anywhere until he gave it to me. He carefully said, "Because I didn't come to you and show you my papers".

Interesting. My son thought his actions were wrong more so because he didn't show me the papers before he signed them instead of him knowing that signing them was wrong.

My *logical discipline* approach continued...

"Did you think anything would happen if your were caught?" My response was now much softer since his own response was so much different from what I'd anticipated.

"No, I was just trying not to get in trouble for not turning my papers in. I forgot to show them to you in time to get them signed. So, I signed them myself."

I assumed my son was trying to be devious, signing my name in order to get out of showing me his grades. I did some thinking and decided to take the logical route. Which, in this case, was asking my son these series of questions to "get the bottom of things", as my mom used to say.

While he *still* did not make the right choice, his decision for doing so was different than what I assumed. (See, the old saying about "assuming" is true.)

Reevaluate the Poor Choice

Now that you have gone through the background information, asked a series of simple questions, or tried reasoning with them, ask yourself if a "correction" is necessary.

So, I decided to stop the questions and explain something to my son. I let him know that signing someone else's name, regardless of your intentions, is wrong. I explained to him that we are a family of honor and integrity.

"What does that mean", he asked. "It means we tell the truth and don't pretend to be someone that we are not. We always do what is right."

"Do you understand that is how we represent our family? With honor and integrity?"

He nodded his head in agreement.

"Your name means something," I continued. "Your honor and integrity protects that value of your name!"

This time, I could see a light bulb turning on. This time, it was in my son's head. He completely understood what I was saying.

If you've covered these logical steps with your child and they're showing a level of understanding, then you've just accomplished the same task an actual "correction"—timeout, grounding, et cetera—would provide. Sometimes an additional correction is still necessary and sometimes it is not. That's your call.

So, in my story with my son, an actual "correction" was unnecessary. He understood the effect of his actions and how to act in the future. It didn't require a "correction", only a conversation.

If you feel that a correction is still necessary, then help your child understand that through their behavior and the logical reasoning that followed, they themselves chose to experience the consequences and that you, as a parent, helped them come to that conclusion instead of doling out a random punishment.

Ah, Now We Are Getting Somewhere!

I'm often asked if I feel my children feel like they are "getting away with it," when I only talk with them about their behavior without giving them a tangible consequence or correction.

The answer is absolutely "No!" They didn't get away with anything. I found out about their wrongdoing, addressed it, helped them show me they understood that their actions were wrong, and we chose to correct it.

My son, in this case didn't need anything more to change his behavior. From that point on, he didn't sign my name. He understood how it was wrong. We discussed it. We addressed it. We changed it. We moved forward. We did it together. With logic.

In addition to his changed behavior, he received a mini life lesson about honor which will guide him in the future.

The goal of discipline is corrected and improved behavior, and if you are seeing improved behavior thanks to your communication, that's all that matters.

The Communication is More Important Than the Correction

My grandfather used to tell me a great story that teaches just that lesson. It goes like this:

A guy traveling quickly through a small town in Georgia (He changed the name of the state each time he told me the story. Which was often.) decided he would slow down rather than actually stop at a stop sign. He didn't realize that a police officer saw this and he was quickly pulled over. The police officer walked up to his window and asked, "Sir, do you know that you didn't come to a complete stop at the stop sign back there?"

The man responded, "Yes, but I did slow down." The police officer proceeded to pull out his night stick and beat the guy over the head! The man yelled "STOP!!!" The officer replied, "Do you want me to stop or do you want me to slow down?"

We can learn something from this story, of course.

Communication here made a literal difference. The man passing through the town tried justifying his actions with a response he probably knew wasn't sufficient. The police officer had to give a real demonstration to communicate the difference.

I'm not condoning violence or beating. That's just a funny, old story that happens to teach the importance of clear communication.

When you and your child communicate clearly and they come to the conclusion that their poor choice shouldn't be repeated, you've taught them the right lesson. Without communication, sending children to their rooms to "think about what they've done," will not give you the results you are hoping for.

What may seem logical to you may not seem that way to them. When your children feel their actions are logical, it's up to you to be the voice of reason.
Strengthen your communication and your children will increase muscle memory to help them make better decisions next time. Let logic lead the way and you'll be amazed at the growth in your children!

Keep at it! It works, it really, really works! But don't take my word for it.

Try it for yourself. And your children. Especially your children.

What My Son Said

Me: "Your homework says to write down a sentence using the word 'simple' in it. But you need have at least 7 words in it."

My son: "Ok..."

"This is very very very very simple!"

Age: 7

CHAPTER 4

There's No Crying In Baseball

Yes, I was one of those dads.

Before my son was born, I already had long-reach dreams of him hitting home-runs at the World Series and getting drafted—hey, possibly first pick—into one of the MLB's biggest teams.

When I was a child, those were my dreams. Those aspirations belonged to me. I was a decently good baseball player and went pretty far in my "career." (Ok, does the end of middle school count?) And my dreams never really completely disappeared.

So when my son was born, and as he grew, I dreamed of the redemption my son would bring to me as he began soaring to the greatest athletic heights imaginable. These dreams of redemption became increasingly fevered, in a way. I pictured in great detail my first-born child's unparalleled athletic power and achievement. Lucrative endorsements would follow rapidly as his incredible skill just got better and better. This would be great for his image and for his confidence, and pretty good for my pride, too. He would even have to turn down major deals because they would be pouring in too fast and furious for him to take all of them.

Ever have a thought like this?

When my son was five years old, it was time. I spent money on a nice glove, a shiny bat, and the soon-to-be dirty cleats worn as he hit home run after home run in his first baseball league. (Can you guess where this story is headed? Keeping reading, this gets good.) His star power would mesmerize the crowds. He'd set records in every single possible category. I just knew that every day, as the sun broke through his little-boy bedroom window, he'd beg and beg with ferocity to grab my heavily used baseball glove to throw the ball back and forth before the school day, after the school day, and for good measure, for the last time in the golden hour of twilight, right before bed, where he would even dream of baseball. The reality of this, however, didn't come to fruition. You're about to see why.

It all started when I signed my son up to a baseball team, filled with excitement. Remember, I knew he was going to be a star. I mean, he was my son. He went to practice, and played in several games. But he spent more time looking at the people in the stands, trying to catch butterflies, and counting how many daffodils he could pick up in the outfield—before three outs forced him back to the dugout. He was already great at making people laugh, so he latched onto that bit instead of learning new baseball skills. Even though I could see that star power deep within him, he didn't pay its possibilities any mind.

Then the Whole Thing Finally Came Crashing Down

The coach didn't usually leave the dugout in the middle of a game. But one time, he did. All of the parents glanced over in his direction as he headed in our direction. We didn't know what was going on.

"Mr. Bultman?" he asked, passing all the other parents, directing his attention solely on me. "Oh, this can't be good," I thought.

I couldn't see the dugout from where I was sitting, so the coach invited me over for a clearer view. On the way to the dugout, the coach's demeanor already told the story. I didn't quite know how it would all play out but I knew it would be revealed soon enough.

I saw my son on the ground. This wasn't good. But he wasn't hurt. At all. "Son, are you ok?" I asked, trying to put the pieces together.

He didn't respond to me, but as he turned around, he had an oh-boy-I'm-caught look on this face. His baseball cleats held him fast to the dugout fence. This wasn't an accident, by the way. My son had—with great skill—tied his long, blue shoelaces to the fence. He could not move and he could not get his feet out. Nor could any adult get his feet out.

He was stuck.

At that point I realized I'd done something terribly wrong. I'm the one who inadvertently put him in that position (figuratively speaking). I never asked my son if he was interested in playing baseball. It was my dream, not his.

After I (eventually) helped get my son's cleats unmangled from the confines of the ball field fence, I realized I had to change my approach to my children's interests. If I spent the rest of my life force-feeding them what they did not want, they would either reject it quickly or do it joylessly. I didn't want that. Something had to give. And it had to start with me. Right away.

I Needed to Make a Change

We should make it a necessary point to discover what interests our children—and not force our own interests upon them, even though we may believe they will love and succeed in those interests if only they try. And trust me, I wanted my son to love baseball. That star potential was slapping me right in the face—even though I seemed to be the only one who could feel it.

Children educate us. While you may have had fantasies about your son or daughter loving just what you did when you were a kid, don't force these aspirations on them. Sometimes it's just not what they're interested in. No matter how much you want them to be.

Sometimes it means letting go of your own childhood dreams—becoming a baseball star, for instance—and instead giving them the support they need to accomplish their own unique goals, those passions that bring them joy and put a sparkle of excitement into their eyes as they work hard to achieve what makes them happy and confident.

Encourage participation in whatever it is they love to do—karate, painting, theater, anything at all. It's all about their interests. Dedicate yourself to helping them be the best they can be at whatever they love to do.

Support them as they grow and find happiness and pride in their own dreams, not the dreams you want them to have, but their very own. And who knows, you might just find a whole new appreciation for their passions yourself. The sooner you learn this, the better off you'll be. Trust me.

Inspire Your Children

Be Realistic

Enter fatherhood knowing that your child is most likely to think differently than you and to have interests different from your own. Do not assume you know what your children enjoy doing. And don't set up expectations—for yourself or your child.

Ask Them

Talk with your children and ask them what they're into—the things that get their attention as they go through their days. You may be surprised at the activities they want to explore. Do not expect that they should like, for instance, playing with Barbie dolls when they'd rather be dribbling a basketball. Don't assume. Incorrect assumptions and unmet expectations lead your child to feel they disappointed you or that you may be angry with them. For instance, your assumptions may get your child tied to a dugout fence with no easy escape. Assumptions don't benefit anyone.

Before you buy baseball cleats, try throwing a ball with them outside first. Before you put them in dance classes, teach them how to do a cartwheel. Before you have them take singing lessons, turn on the radio and see how they respond in the car.

This helps. And will make things easier for you later.

Guide Them

Don't forget to help guide them through their decisions. If they want to try something new, explain how they'll be spending their time when they choose to pursue their particular interest. Tell them the good, the bad, and everything in between. Explain the commitment they are making. Make sure they understand it, buy into it, and want to move forward. Then let them decide. Avoid bias and the attempt to sway them in any particular direction.

Set Limits

While you do want to let your children's interests flourish, you may need or want to set certain limitations when it comes to a new activity. Maybe budget restraints take horse-riding out of the picture. Perhaps the fear of dangerous football injuries will influence your decision to keep your child off the field. Communicate these limits as soon as possible.

Be Flexible

Understand that once you discuss these things with your children and get their feedback, when it comes to their choices, you need to be flexible and understanding. Support them. Love them. Be there for them no matter what.

Adapt with Them

If your child is into something, try learning more about why they're so taken with the activity or subject. You may find that when you take an interest yourself, you get to learn about and adapt to their interests—which is a wonderful tool that allows for valuable bonding time.

Remain Well-Rounded

You want to help your children pursue their interests, but you also want to make sure they discover and explore a variety of them. If your children's interests involve video games and only video games, it's wise to suggest outdoor family fun every now and then.

Try Again

It's alright to ask your child if they've rekindled an interest in something they once wanted no part of. They may be excited you ask. They may want to go for it again. But be careful to let them know it's okay if they're still averse to the activity. Don't make them feel badly about it if they're not interested. But sometimes, as their personalities change, they'll want to give it another shot.

Do You Ever Hear Children Say, "Dad, I Want to Disappoint You?"

Of course not. Most children try things simply because you want them to. They do look up to you, after all. Take that knowledge as motivation to feed into their real interests and you will find that their success rate in those areas will be far greater than anything you might have expected when swaying them to follow your desires. Use your dad power for good.

Since the time of our "dugout incident," I have learned to place my son's interests ahead of mine. And the results have been phenomenal.

He has played on a soccer team and a basketball team. He's learned how to skate, swim unassisted, ride his bike without training wheels, catch bugs, wrestle frequently, run with the dog—and much, much more.

Right now, he's signed up to Cub Scouts. He loves the camping, the BB guns, the archery, the lessons and the fun. I'm not sure how long he will have an interest in Scouts, but for now, he loves it. Which means...I love it!

I'm letting him explore his interests by the handful. Whatever he wants to do, as long as it is safe and reasonable, I allow him to do it.

Letting them try new things lets me learn something new as a dad.

I learned that it is a great thing for him to have unique interests and try activities I never participated in while I was growing up. His love for all kinds of random things previously unknown to me helps me try new things with him. Now, as I think more closely about his passions, I even begin to reevaluate my own. This has helped me assist him in cultivating new hobbies and bonding with him as we participate in new activities I otherwise wouldn't have tried.

Like our recent camping trip with my son's Cub Scouts. I didn't go camping while I was growing up, so I wasn't too comfortable with it. Let's just say that my idea of camping is very limited—more like a Hilton on the beach than a sleeping bag in a tent. But since my son is into it, the whole family headed to a sports store together. We bought a massive tent, sleeping bags and everything that goes along with the experience (which is A LOT, by the way) and headed out camping for the weekend. We went camping in November. It was freezing cold but my son had a blast. Which meant that I had a blast. My whole family did. If we'd ignored or been less supportive of his interest, we would have missed out on making such great memories together.

Your children's interests help develop new interests in life and in yourself.

This can only be done if you are truly interested in your children.

Dugout Do-Over

Almost three years after my son attempted to play baseball, he asked me about playing again. I spent some time talking about the last time we attempted baseball. He looked a little puzzled, and barely remembered the amusing moment when his little self could not get free of the dugout fence. While it's a funny story today, it certainly wasn't funny then. I told him that I would support his choice but I cautioned him to think it through, take it slow, and make his own decision.

That night, he opted for us to play "catch" in the backyard.

It was a good day for a dad's dream to come true, if only for a moment.

CHAPTER 5

Making Bedtime Sweet: A Recipe You'll Love

"I'm hungry!"

My children say this to me often. Very frequently. Ok, ok… they say this to me, like everyday. You've heard this too. You've even said this yourself.

It is a phrase that warrants action. Every day, parents have to decide what they're going to feed their children. Then we have to actually do it.

My children are smart. When I hear the combined sound of soft footsteps and the pantry door opening, I know what's up. My children often sneak into the kitchen, right around dinner time, to browse through the food options in preparation to share their opinions on just what might be a good idea for dinner that evening. They know that if they get to me before I start dinner there's a chance they'll get what they want. Sometimes they do. Sometimes they don't. It depends on the day. And how busy I am. And how hungry I am (which is directly related to my mood. More on that later.).

Normally, I have a go-to mental list of dinner options that fulfill two missions: smooth, efficient preparation and a yummy dinner the kids will love. It's a routine that works for all of us.

Until It Doesn't

One evening, my children came to me with earnest expressions and began begging me to let them help with dinner. I looked at them saying "You don't even know how to make dinner."

They said "Yes, we do!"

"No, you don't," I quickly replied.

"Yes, we do!" they fired back.

"No, you…" Wait.

Why was I in a battle to convince my children they didn't know how to cook? They'd already convinced themselves that they did. Who was I to not at least let them give it a shot.

So, on this night, after about five minutes of bargaining and pleading on their end, I finally caved.

This is totally because I'm the "cool dad." Or maybe it was because I was too hungry to argue anymore. I'll leave that one up to you.

I let them help with dinner.

I'm Not Worried

Since my children are in elementary school, as we make dinner, I'm careful about what I let them do. I'm not worried about them spilling things. They tend to be pretty careful. I'm also not worried about them burning themselves on a hot stove. They're cautious—and they know the ramifications of mixing curiosity with high temperatures.

Wait. I Am Worried

What am I worried about? How to guide them through the process. They don't know the steps it takes to make edible food—I mean, a delicious meal. (After all, they've never cooked dinner before.) Most times I don't even have a grasp on those steps.

But We Manage

As a dad, it's my job to lay out clear instructions so my children learn, every day, how to do something new—and enjoy the process at the same time. So, we work together, and follow a recipe designed to fulfill every element of the perfect meal—delectable food, great conversation, and satisfied appetites all around.

I'm getting somewhere with this, I promise. What other routines do parents and children go through every day?

(Hint, it usually happens after dinner.)

Your Children's Bedtime Routine!

Cooking and bedtime routines are more similar than you'd imagine. Let's start with cooking. We have the ingredients, the instructions, the preparation, and the fulfillment. This is the core flow for a meal—a basic family meal. (We aren't talking about running five-star restaurants here.) Without these steps, dinner is out of sync. It may not taste right, and most importantly, your children won't be satisfied. And if your children are anything like mine, you know they will tell you when they don't like their meal.

So this whole flow is very important for dinner, and for... bedtimes.

(Don't go to sleep on me just yet...)

Instructions: Read Entire Recipe Before You Begin.

Ingredients May Vary

All kinds of ingredients make up a great bedtime routine in the same way that all kinds of ingredients make up a great meal.

When you're cooking, ingredients and prep times vary depending on the dish. That doesn't make one dish better than another. It's just different. So when it comes to getting your children ready for bedtime, the same formula applies.

The best ingredients depend on the child you have and you've got to find the ones sure to satisfy your child every time.

Remember, don't focus on a rigid set of steps for each child. Instead, direct your attention to what works best for your child's unique personality.

Just like cooking, it's all in the mix.

The List. It's All About the List

Jot down the core bedtime ingredients. I've also included some creative motivations so you can explain to your children why they're doing what they're doing. These may include:

- **Showers or baths**—so they get rid of the stinkies. Because they take playing in the dirt very seriously.
- **Laying out clothes for the next day**—so they match. At least sometimes.
- **Reading a bedtime story**—so they can laugh and learn and have fun with you before they go to sleep.
- **Cleaning your room**—so they learn the basics of responsibility.
- **Planning for the next day**—so they learn that staying ahead always beats out playing the catch up game.
- **Talking about the day you had**—so they always have a time to speak. Because what they say matters, too.
- **Saying prayers and giving thanks**—so they learn why they are blessed and learn there is always something to be thankful for. Even on bad days.

Your customized list of ingredients are the things your children should complete in order to fall asleep. They may be a portion of this list or you may have additional ingredients specific to your family. Give this some thought. This list is important.

Know the Full List of Ingredients

Be sure your children know this list. That means that you need to know the list. Know it well. Be sure you know the best way to help them remember the list. If they're more verbal, you may simply need to tell them. If they're more visual, write the list on a board so they can check off their progress. Tap into your creative side to discover the perfect bedtime recipe for your one-of-a-kind child. Serve up the ingredients spoonful by spoonful or let them bite right into the full course. Whatever it is, be on the same page.

You may need a few methods to ensure your children know the list—and that they follow it.

Here's Why

One evening, as I did every evening, I asked my children to brush their teeth. My daughter went in, brushed her teeth, came out and let me smell her breath as proof. (Yes, it may be weird, but you know you do it, too. Admit it.)

Then my son went into the bathroom to brush his teeth. He came out five minutes later—after I'd called for him. I asked to smell his breath. Um, let's just say that this turned out to be a bad thing. At least on this night.

When he went into the bathroom, he got sidetracked by a toy he saw on the ground. He hadn't even remembered that I'd asked him to brush his teeth. When I asked him again, he went back in and accomplished this task the second time around.

It was obvious I needed a new way to get my children to brush their teeth. A better method. A reason they'd understand and be interested in. So. I came up with some catchphrases like the ones I noted above.

Teach Your Child About Each Ingredient

What is the Ingredient, Exactly?

Instead of describing your ingredient with the obvious name—"Brushing your teeth," for instance—develop more creative phrases to make the activity more fun and easy to understand. "Brushing your cavities away," for example, brings more clarity to the purpose.

I asked my daughter once, "Are you fully prepared for the future?"

Was this a deep conversation? Nope. Nothing like that. What was I really saying to her?

"Have you laid out your clothes for tomorrow?"

She knew what I meant. Preparing for the future of tomorrow's outfit! Ah, the purpose! See what we did here?

Why is the Ingredient Important?

If you leave out an ingredient, everything changes. The same goes for a missed bedtime ingredient. If you leave something out, you change the comfort of your children's sleeping experience. Sound a little overboard? Children like routine. For example, if you have an overly organized child, they may feel stressed going to bed with a messy room. Skipping the "clean your room" ingredient can change their night. Don't skip important ingredients—and all the ingredients are important.

Some of us have sneaky ones who may to try to skip an ingredient on purpose. Why? Because they don't know why they're doing it. They don't know the value of the ingredient. So watch for sneakiness and add explanations where needed. They'll be less likely to try and get out of an ingredient if they know why it's on the list. Afterall, you don't want anyone left with a bitter taste in their mouths about bedtime, do you?

I know I don't.

How Will the Ingredient Be Used?

When your child asks a question, don't say, "Because dad said so!" (See my later chapter about things I won't say to my children.) That's not an explanation. Your children are not always being disrespectful because they ask questions.

They usually ask because they don't know the answer—and they expect their dads to teach them. Communicate with them in a way they'll understand. Explain why the actions you are asking them to take will help them.

For instance, "brushing your cavities away," every night will ensure they'll still have teeth when they're old and gray. A clean room in the morning ensures they'll feel ready for the day. You came up with their unique list because it benefits them and their comfort.

Show them how the ingredients work and why they were created in the first place. This way they know why they're doing what they're doing and why it's important. They'll enjoy it that much more, too. Get their buy-in. It always pays off in the long run.

What Happens if the Ingredient isn't Used?

It is important to communicate consistency and purpose. When your actions have a purpose and you follow through with them consistently, you will see positive progress. For example, the "read before bed" ingredient serves a purpose. It improves reading. When you read with your children consistently, they start to read faster and will continue to enjoy longer and more complex books. Explaining—and proving— the benefits shows your children what they will miss if they don't use the ingredient, and what they gain when they do use them. For example, my children and I have seen the benefits of growth in their personal prayer time. We pray for various people and situations and we see how those prayers come to fruition. My children love experiencing that.

Put All the Ingredients Together

No chef prepares a dish the same way. Each possesses different steps, different styles, and different amounts of time to bring the meal to completion. Your children's bedtime routines are no different.

Steps

At this point, you've already communicated the ingredients your child needs for a sweet bedtime routine. Pay close attention to which ingredients are used first and in what order. Some children need an ordered list. Others just need a general one. With options like these, you can keep bedtime an interesting and evolving experience. Switch from an ordered list to a more general one as your children get older or want more responsibility. And you can keep the steps in order, of course, because some children simply need or find comfort in a specifically ordered list of steps.

Style

Make sure you choose bedtime ingredients customized to your children's unique personalities and interests. You may want to foster growth in writing with one child while your other children focus on reading. It is important to note here that "style" is all about those details that aren't on the list of "must have" ingredients. Brushing your teeth, for instance, should be on every list of bedtime ingredients, no matter what your children's style is. Right?

Time

Children complete things at different rates. Knowing your children is especially important here because you do not want to rush an overly detailed child and conversely, you don't want to stall a child trying to take advantage of staying up as late as they can stretch it. For those children who need defined barriers, set a timeline for them. If you have a really detailed child, set a stopwatch so there are no disputes as to whether or not the time countdown was accurate (that goes out to all of the little negotiators out there, like my son).

Fulfillment

We all love this part—when the meal is ready to serve and it's time to dive into great food with great company. You anticipate the spices, the textures, and the overall full sensory satisfaction and enjoyment you will have of each and every bite.

Oh, my children don't always like going through their set of ingredients, but when they are showered, comfortable, and cozy—wrapped up with me and enjoying a story or a last-minute TV show, they are completely satisfied. It's during this moment that we all enjoy the full satisfaction of a bedtime routine well-done. This is the perfect time to remind them why the routine works.

That's when children will start to anticipate and look forward to incorporating all of their bedtime ingredients, too. They know what they are and why they're doing them. Your children have bought into the benefits and are ready to enjoy them—and so are you.

Sweet Satisfaction

I'm very consistent with my children's bedtime routine. They know the ingredients and we have no disputes on the process. None. We have the perfect process. One-hundred-percent of the time. All the time. Okay, okay...we're getting better by the day. We work to get better. That's what matters.

One of Our Ingredients is "Bedtime Prayer"

I pray with my children every night. We've been doing this since they were two-years-old and barely understood the concept of prayer.

And while I am very consistent, there are times when even dads don't remember everything (even though my son thinks I'm a superhero and I couldn't possibly forget something). I do pretend that I'm Rambo sometimes, remember?

One night, I turned off the lights in my son's room and walked out. I was done with daddy duty and it was on to other things. It wasn't even two minutes later I heard a quiet whisper. My son. This time, he was speaking in a quiet voice, one that was rather rare around our house. I couldn't make out what he was saying, but as I got closer, the words became more clear.

"Will you say prayers with me, dad?"

My son was making sure we used the ingredients we set. When we started this routine at age two, it didn't make sense to him. Over the course of five years, it was not only something we did, but a "must have" ingredient. He does not go to sleep until we say prayers together.

(No matter how much you plan on teaching your children about life, about love, about happiness, about what's right and wrong, you get "schooled" from your own students—your sons or daughters. And it puts a smile on your face. Because you're proud.)

I missed an important ingredient that night. He needed the final portion of the perfect bedtime meal—the warm comfort of a nourishing prayer. With dad. I was part of that ingredient. It was he who taught me that night. After we said prayers, and he was fast asleep, I felt thankful for the person my son was becoming. And it all started with an ingredient. One that I set and he followed.

No matter what ingredients you choose, make sure they have importance—and that you understand the importance. Start off instilling these important values into your children at a young age. The younger, the better. The more consistent you are, the sweeter your bedtime routine will be.

So. Hold your pan tight. Grab the skillet firmly. Adjust your daddy chef's hat—and get ready to enjoy sweet bedtime success for your children, and for yourself.

Bon appetit, dads!

What My Son Said

Me: "I love you!"

My son: "I love you more than all the grains of rice, all the grains of sand, and all the parrots in paradise!!!"

Age: 6

CHAPTER 6

Tea, Tiaras & Fairytales

Once upon a time…(hey, why not?). Once upon a time in a land far, far away (okay, it was about two hours away), my best friend held a birthday party for his little girl. She was seven-years-old, and to my best friend, she was the most beautiful princess in all the land. It's a feeling all dads share about their daughters. As best friend, I came to celebrate. Lots of little ones, especially girls, ran around at full speed, giggling and having a complete blast. It was adorable. Really.

After the requisite (and complete highlight of every birthday party) cake and ice cream, the girls wanted to play dress-up, paint nails, and put on makeup. They aimed to hit that princess-in-the-castle beauty- thing that all little girls long for. You know, the typical things most little girls like to do.

As I stood watching the girls with my friend, I had no idea that I'd suddenly become a target. I looked over at him. He looked over at me. I noticed a glint of delight in his eye. Jokingly, my friend asked if I would like to join in the fun with the girls.

"Really?" I said, with more-than-a-little sarcasm.

To his surprise and mine, without a second thought, I jumped right in and soon enough was completely involved in their infectious little-girl energy and antics. I let the young girls paint my fingernails day-glo pink and load my eyelashes up with layers upon layers of mascara (and ahem, I have pretty long eyelashes already...so you can imagine I looked very, very pretty).

There's more.

They applied tons of blue and pink–especially pink–eyeshadow, about 50 layers of sparkling red lipstick and even more bright pink blush.

(I even have the picture to prove it, by the way.)

When the makeover was over, I basically looked colorful. Really, really, really *colorful*. The girls were BEYOND thrilled. Once I was done up and looked "sooooooo pretty!!!", cameras flashed endlessly as my friend caught every angle and every pose, laughing the whole time, saying over and over, "you're going to regret this later!" I don't fully recall if these were all real pictures, or just mental ones. But either way, he enjoyed the sight of it all.

To my surprise, though, I didn't regret it. Not really. Why?

My own daughter.

I decided I'd take the same approach with her. To jump right in. Without embarrassment. To have makeup applied to my face and polish applied to my nails frequently. To play her favorite games with her, and have tea with her, and to be vulnerable and have fun at the same time.

When you're a dad, having a daughter calls for a gentle, exacting, delicate and very careful kind of love. A love that, if you really want to make the best of it, requires you to do all the non-dad-

like things so very often—makeup, tea time, dress-up, PINK—
that to your daughter, they actually ARE very dad-like things.

I'm dedicating this chapter to all the dads out there who have
little girls.

Girls. Who put "do not enter" signs on their doors. Who spend
hours organizing their makeup (even the young ones). Who
take combing their dolls' hair *very* seriously, the ones who talk
about little girl drama at the school playground. Who take
"make-believe" to a whole new level. This goes out to dads like
me who've experienced all of this first-hand.

If you have a daughter, you understand what I mean when I say
that there really are no words to describe why or how having a
daughter is one of the best bonds a dad can have. It just is. You
have to experience it. But you have to work at it. You have to
be careful. Daughters are special. You have to pay a lot of close
attention.

It's The Little Things

Over the years, I've learned what connects me best with my
daughter. Most times it's the little things. And when I say
"little things," I mean they seem "little" to me. But they are
tremendously important to my daughter. When we do these
things—share a cup of tea, together, for instance—my daughter
feels closer to me, and we are more connected. This connection
strengthens our already-tight relationship. And with every
"little thing" we do together, to her, these actions speak just as
loudly as the words themselves, perhaps even louder. They say,
"I love you."

The Little Things I Do to Connect with My Little Girl

Have a Cup of Tea. And Drink the Whole Cup

I'll be honest. For a long time, I had a sneaking suspicion that tea time really wasn't "fun-time" for my daughter. But the truth was, I didn't find it fun. When I saw her crestfallen face the first time I told her I didn't want to have tea with her, I knew I'd been wrong. Since then, I won't turn down a sweet cup of make-believe tea. The memories will always be far sweeter than the tea.

Let Her Make-You-Up. Heavily

Dads, we need to change the way we think of the term "manly." As a dad, I think men are much manlier when they lay down and let their daughters glamour up their faces with makeup. I guarantee you will make your daughter's face glow with a smile far brighter than the glitter-pink lipstick on your own face. Encourage her to document it, too!

Play Dress-Up. And Wear Anything

Bows, ribbons, clip-on earrings, gowns, and tiaras. Whatever the accessory necessary, take the time to visit magical castles in faraway lands and battle creatures of unknown places. Playing dress-up with your daughter will not only show her that you are giving her your full attention, but it will help enrich her creative imagination. Do this, and you will be her knight in shining armor.

Brush Your Daughter's Hair. With Joy

Getting your daughter ready to go somewhere is not a woman's job. It's a parent's job, which makes it a dad's job. That means men need to step up and be active with their daughter and their care. Brush your daughter's hair daily. Do it to help get her ready to go somewhere and whether you're going somewhere or not, brushing your daughter's hair is not only very comforting for her, it can also evoke any number of conversations and deepen your communication and connection with her.

Help Choose Her Outfits. And Provide Feedback

Every night before bedtime, my daughter and I pick out her outfit for the next day. (It's one of our bedtime "ingredients".) This allows us to work together as a team and also shows me what looks she is interested in. The older she gets, the more I let her take the lead in picking out her clothes. And because of this, she has started asking me my thoughts on what she is picking out. We have learned a lot about each other!

Read Her a Book. Regularly

One incredible way to grab your daughter's attention is to read her a book. Reading does a lot of great things. First, it provides one-on-one time together. Secondly, it allows you to be in close physical contact, which is a great bonding experience. Lastly and most importantly, it shows your daughter that you are doing something specifically for her.

Let Her Sit on Your Lap. Anytime

I bond with my daughter through physical connection. Having my daughter "snuggle" with me during a movie, while I read her a book, or just talking about our day builds our ever-growing bond. I've started telling her that I need that time with her and I know she craves to have that time to capture my attention.

Tell Her that You Love Her. Constantly

I tell my daughter frequently and randomly that I love her. Each time I tell her, she blushes. I'm doing this for both of us. I know that it melts her heart and it also makes me stop and really think how much I care for her. I tell her randomly because I don't want her thinking I was only telling her because I have to at the appropriate times—at bedtime, for example, or when she's leaving for school for the day. I could be making dinner and I may tell her out loud across the house. She always yells back, "I love you, too!!"

Let Her Tell You Anything. And I Mean, Anything!

I'm a big believer in letting your children tell you anything. I don't care if it's good, bad, or unintentionally hurtful. My children know from experience that they can tell me anything about anything. And, since girls talk more than boys on average, it's important that I give her a platform that allows her to do just that. Daughters are fascinating. If you learn to listen, they'll learn to tell you anything. And everything.

Ask Her Questions. All Kinds of Them

In addition to being an open window and telling your daughter she can tell you anything she wants, she also loves it when you ask her questions. This stimulates great conversation and they feel like they are getting a lot of attention. So. Start with the easy ones, like:

- "How was your day?"
- "What was your favorite part of your day?"
- "What would you like to do tomorrow?"

Ask open-ended questions. And just listen as your girls let loose on the answer portion.

Blow Her a Kiss. Then Smile

Blowing your daughter a kiss has a lot of the same effects as giving her a hug. But, this is an action of love you can do from across the room, as she is running up to her classroom, or as she drives away in a car. I will make a personal guarantee that this action has a positive impact on your daughter's perception of you. It simply shows love.

Write Her a Letter. Have Her Write You Back

My daughter writes me a lot of letters. At age 5, she is limited with what she communicates but she puts full effort into every note. And she smiles ear-to-ear when I read them. She loves it. Conversely, writing a letter to your daughter may even yield greater emotions. She will read it in front of you and a million times when you are not there. Realize the impact it has on her, even if it's not apparent to you at first. Keep at it. The impact is huge.

Take Her Out on a Date. Let Her Pick the Destination

Taking your daughter out on a date is particularly important if you have more than one child. Take the time to interact with her in other ways we've already mentioned in preparation for the date, such as picking out her clothes, brushing her hair, and putting a little makeup on her (not you) this time. Make it a special occasion. Let her help pick where you are going. Document your fun. Show her the pictures and talk about it later. These are memories in the making.

Hold Her Hand. Proudly

When I'm out in public, I often ask for my daughter to hold my hand. I do this more than just for her protection. I want her to know that I want to be affectionate with her in public. I want her to see that I want a connection with her no matter where we are and no matter who is around. Plus, it makes her feel safe and helps build confidence. Besides, who wouldn't want to be attached to their sweet daughter?

Real Men Put Their Girls First

It is easy for men to read this list and brush them off as a woman's job. It is. I've done it before. Don't. Just don't do it. A real man puts his daughter first. He carefully considers and cares deeply about her thoughts, her emotions, and her temperament. He helps guide her. He is there for her through everything. Really there. He's her touchstone. Her sounding board. He is patient and kind. He is what love is.

Your role as a father is so important to your daughter—to who she is now and to the person she will become. The time is always now to step up and connect with your little girl before she's not a little girl anymore.

The connection points listed above are just several of many ways to connect with your daughter. Think of what your daughter loves and add those activities to the list. Think of what she needs. You're her first and most indelible example of what it means to be a man, to be a father, and to be a human being. For her, be a good one.

Once Upon a Time (An Especially Sweet Time)

My daughter sat in my lap as we talked about her day. This happens all the time, but there's a reason, you'll soon see, why I'm telling you about this particular sitting-on-the-lap-time and-talking-about-her-day day.

She told me what she did in school, including the mini-drama between the kids on the playground along with what she wanted to wear to school tomorrow. I have to admit, I was probably enjoying our time together more than she was. I was just amazed at how much she was willing and wanting to tell me.

Later in the conversation, I stopped her.

I said, "Why do you tell me so much?"

She responded with, "Because you love me, daddy!"

Wow.

Just like that, everything we did together. All the fun we had. All the special times we shared. All the affection. All the love. It all made complete sense.

And worth every single minute of it.

What My Son Said

My son: (In a loud voice) "I HATE this game!"

Me: "Please say it politely"

My son: (In a quiet voice) "I hate this game."

Age: 6

CHAPTER 7

Don't Say It. Just. Don't. Say. It.

Words are powerful. Very.

As a very young man (still just a college freshman, in fact), I snagged an interview at a high-end marketing company. I had the skill. I had the desire. I found a company and I went after it! That's right, I was confident. My work was pretty solid—packed full of some pretty major accomplishments and an impressive portfolio (again, for someone my age).

Some of these included:

- Individual school websites built for the area district. (Uh-huh, this was big!)
- Freelance website design for satisfied clients. (Yes, there's the experience!)
- Visually designed websites for a small dental firm. (Yep, I had the skill!)

With portfolio in hand, sweaty palms, and a new tie knotted to perfection, I walked into the office ready to prove my worth. What did I have to lose? I had everything to lose. In my mind, anyway.

Half an hour of heart-racing waiting later, an intimidating adult emerged. He looked powerful. He dressed the part. He looked the part. And he acted... Well, without even looking at me, he conferred with the receptionist and left. A few minutes passed. And a few minutes more. He then came into the waiting room again—and invited me into his intimidating office.

His office was pretty amazing. I'll give him that, for sure. A sleek and simple wooden desk. Modern. Oh, the lines on the desk fit the shape of the room like a glove. Tasteful pictures in square wooden frames lined up to perfection on the far wall. And the frames complemented the desk to a tee. Remember, I am (and was) in the creative field. I notice things. How they look. How they fit in. What works. What doesn't. Appearances can tell a whole story about a person. They speak, so to speak. And this guy's story was all about power and control. So, naturally, his opinion mattered to me. A lot.

He gave my resume and client list a swift once-over. Keyword is swift. He stared at it for another minute. Another moment is more like it. I could practically hear the silence. He tossed my portfolio on his desk with a sigh of resignation.

I was young. Fresh meat, if you will, in the business world. I took what I heard (or didn't hear) seriously. And sometimes a little too much to heart. I was supposed to, right? I was supposed to take every word I heard from the "experts" as gospel. Especially this guy, the CEO of this company. His power and confidence told me I had to. But did I really need to?

He then punctuated it all with a lecture. It's one of an adult's favorite pastimes. And now it was my turn.

I didn't know it was coming, although a more experienced

person probably would have read the signs. But then again, my lack of experience was part of the reason a lecture started in the first place. Either way, the lecture hit me harder than Mike Tyson's fist to a punching bag. Or a car hitting a brick wall. Anyway, you get the point.

The lecture:

I was too young to be in the marketing industry. (Really?) I should take a job at the local fast-food chain down the road. (What?) I would be "lucky" to get a job in this field later on in life. (For real?) He didn't even give me a chance to speak. And, I didn't. Because again, I was supposed to listen. I was supposed to be attentive. And take every word and run with it. Right?

I was heart-broken. Though I was close to tears, I did the proper thing. I extended my hand and gave him my firmest handshake, thanked him for his time, and left, completely defeated.

I learned a lot about business that day.

But I Learned More About Being a Dad

How? It's like this. Words cannot be taken back, no matter how much we wish they could. Words matter. Big time. So be careful with them. They can be used for good or evil. And there are certain words and behaviors you need to steer clear of when communicating with your children—this is vitally important.

What you say and do affects their confidence, their attitude, their drive and their sense of self-worth. Words and ideas, as has once been said, have the power to change the world.

What adults say has a big impact on young people. For instance, that CEO's words affected me. For awhile, I didn't even want to go to another interview. My self-confidence took a serious blow. I doubt he was even aware that his words would have such a big effect on me, but they did. And it wasn't a good one. Dads, you need to always be aware of what you're saying. Always. Because your children always notice.

Give your children the power to change the world around them so that it's one of confidence and hope and wonder and safety. Dads, your influence on your children—through your words and actions—are right now shaping how they feel about themselves and how they behave in the world.

That's how much your words and behaviors influence your children. While it may seem daunting, it isn't so hard. Just remember how much you love your children. And that your words matter! More than anything.

Just Don't

That interview. I remember it like it was yesterday. I remember getting ready. I remember my sweaty palms. I was so excited. Filled with anticipation. I remember the forever-long waiting in the waiting room (the term "waiting room" made much more sense after my visit).

And, I remember all of the devastating comments that came my way that day. The words were so strong and so unkind. They really, really hurt. I felt defeated.

But only for a time.

After I became a dad and as conversations with my children became more and more important, that day often came back to my memory. I remembered what it felt like to be on the receiving end of harsh words from an adult. I was determined to make sure my children didn't ever hear words like that come out of my mouth.

So I came up with a few phrases that I positively, absolutely, without a shadow of a doubt, do not, under any circumstances, say to my children. This way, I know my words will uplift my children instead of tearing down even the smallest bit of self-confidence. I won't be tearing down any walls. It's just not going to happen. Not once. Not ever.

So, here is my short list. This list is important to me. Very.

1. "I'm busy right now!"

I never say this to my children. Sure, I may actually be busy. But telling your children this is not good. It makes them feel unimportant.

Just like "time is money" when it comes to business, to me, when it comes to fatherhood, I have a new and more important mantra—"time is love." No gift, no tussle on the head, absolutely nothing about fatherhood is more important than giving the precious, irretrievable gift of time to your children.

When your children get to enjoy laughter and talks and fun and hugs and even games of catch with their father—this is what elevates their spirits, strengthens their hearts, gives them confidence and security, and most of all, lets them know that they are loved and important and matter in this world.

We certainly don't want to "waste our money" in business when we let mismanaged plans slip by without a nickel to show for it. And we don't want to "waste our love" with poorly planned schedules that leave our children out of our lives too often. NEVER "fit" your children into your schedule. ALWAYS make sure your schedule revolves around your children.

Your children are beyond the capacity of a word like "worth" or "wealth." They are your best "asset." And they're your greatest treasure. Treat them like gold. Because that's what they are.

2. "Don't bother me!"

When it comes to the word bother, you're telling your children they're causing you trouble, that you would prefer NOT to be bothered, which by definition means to "take the trouble to do something." You're telling them that they're injecting trouble into your life when you "have to" stop that important thing you're doing and show them the attention they need from you. Trouble? Is that really what they're doing—causing you trouble?

As many children have often said (in teenage years most likely), "I didn't ASK to be born!" And it's true. Your children came into this world without request or demand and in return, were born to parents meant to protect, teach, love and nourish them.

From the moment they are born to the time they are able to care for themselves, your guidance is meant to allow them to live their young lives without worry, care or stress. They need you. They, before anyone or anything, deserve the advice and help they seek when they come to you with questions or requests or anything at all. They rely on this. And it's your paramount job as a dad to give them the attention they deserve to get by in their worlds.

Understand your children's needs. Be patient with them. If you require time for yourself or are wrapped up with obligations that keep you from devoting them with your immediate attention, simply explain this. They usually understand.

Don't be dismissive. When you begin asking them not to bother you—especially when they're very young and especially when it's very often, they simply won't come to you for anything. Make them a priority. Lovingly let them know that you'll be there for them as soon as possible. Promise them. And follow through.

3. "You don't understand!"

Since one of your most important roles as a dad is to educate your children, when you tell them they "don't understand," you've failed them as a teacher. A lack of understanding doesn't always fall on the lap of a child, it rests on the shoulders of the parent.

Understanding. The word itself is wrapped up in all kinds of ambiguities, abstractions and points of view confusing to both children and adults.

Children may truly be simply too young to properly conceive an abstract explanation or a metaphorical comparison to let them know why they don't know how to properly code software—okay, that's probably not the common conversation you're likely to have with your child, but you never know.

Our children have unique minds and thought patterns of their own, not to mention their own stages of learning development. Barriers do exist when it comes to the ability to grasp an idea. From specific age sets to learning disabilities to emotional issues and beyond, there are quite often limiting factors that may be out of your control.

But guess what? As the dad, you have the power, knowledge, love, patience, bond and creativity to help them figure out any number of ways—unique to their special selves—to find answers to questions they don't understand. Teach them!

4. "You're not ready!"

So you tell your child they aren't "ready." Did they forget to tie their shoelaces? Is the table not set? Did you create an expectation for them that they had no idea existed? "Not ready" simply means that they were not prepared. There's a difference. If they learn what to do, they'll be ready to do it.

If they've been taught all about a certain subject and have been prepared for their upcoming test, they're ready! How can you trust your child if you haven't involved them and walked them through certain situations to prove they're prepared (and ready!)

to be trusted in whatever that setting may be?

Maybe the statement has more to do with you than your children. Perhaps you've told your children this because you're not ready to invest the time necessary to prepare them to be "ready" for whatever opportunities, desires and obstacles await them.

Understand the desires of your children's hearts. When you do—and when you invest your time in their precious lives—you prepare them for all the myriad and unexpected situations life will offer them—both now and when they're grown.

5. "You can't do it."

Why? Do you have an answer? Don't you believe in them? Don't you trust them? Have you shown them how to do it—whatever it is? The answer? You. You and all the lessons they've learned from you. You're their dad. Your job is to teach them HOW or at least help them believe they CAN.

Even if your children fail, time and time again, tell them over and over and over:

- "You CAN do it"
- "YOU can do it!"
- "You can DO it!"
- "You can do IT!"

Believing in them, being proud of their courage to try and try and try, cheering them on no matter what—it builds their confidence, their sense of self-worth, the belief that "THEY

CAN DO IT."

Do you want confident, positive and courageous children? Then speak confidently to them and reinforce how much you believe in them, their potential and their courage.

6. "Choose something easier!"

Don't teach your children to take the easy way out. If they heed your advice, they may never get anywhere. They may also get the idea that you didn't believe they could do any better. But if you encourage what looks like a daunting goal—one that your child might not gain—they'll get stronger every time they try to reach it. And when they do reach a big goal or a seemingly impossible dream, it will only reinforce what they've already learned from you—work hard, put your mind to it and you can do anything you want.

Why not use the phrase "choose something harder"? Challenge your children. Let them know you believe they can do more than they think they can. Teach them to test their abilities instead of taking the easy way out.

So. Let's run down a few examples of some dreams your child might share with you. Do they want to become a doctor? Tell them to prepare for a lot of studying, but not that the coursework will be too hard for them and they'll drop out because they just can't hack it. Do your children want to start their own company? Don't tell them that there will be a lot of growing pains and letdowns!

Share with them the successes and possibilities and excitement of such an endeavor. Are your children having problems reading a book? Sit with them and help them sound out words. Don't choose a lower reading level!

Strengthen your children by helping them. Help them by giving them your time. Give them your time and teach them life's most important priorities.

Simple Game. Real Lesson

When I was about ten, my brother and I played a certain game. We loved it. Each of us would ball a fist and lightly tap on each other's shoulder. The first tap didn't hurt at all. Neither did the second, the third, fourth, or even the twentieth. But over the course of about ten minutes, our shoulders started to get a little sore. Then ten minutes after that, every slight tap just hurt.

So while the words you say may seem harmless—just like that light tapping over and over and over that my brother and I shared as children—your comments have the same effect. After just a little while, even the smallest, seemingly innocuous verbal jab just hurts.

Words are that powerful. They either build up your children or they break them down, one syllable at a time. Such passing comments, said more out of thoughtlessness than harm, don't seem to hurt when your children hear them—at first, anyway.

Over time, small comments and phrases and words have an indelible impact on your children. Even if they can't articulate their feelings yet, such words can build a wedge between you and your children. And when they do finally have the words, the wedge may become a chasm.

Make sure that doesn't happen. Speak life into your children. Speaking life into your children means you are focused on raising your children in a way that always encourages, always strengthens, always hopes for the best, always prepares for anything, always creates a bond and always displays reliability.

So speak life. Speak love. Words matter. Use them responsibly.

Replace Your Phrases

DON'T SAY: "I'm busy right now!"
DO SAY: "What's on your mind?"

DON'T SAY: "Don't bother me!"
DO SAY: "For you, anything!"

DON'T SAY: "You don't understand!"
DO SAY: "Let me teach you!"

DON'T SAY: "You're not ready."
DO SAY: "I believe in you!"

DON'T SAY: "You can't do it."
DO SAY: "You can do ANYTHING you put your mind to!"

DON'T SAY: "Choose something easier."
DO SAY: "Are you ready for a challenge?"

This way you're addressing their needs just as every dad should.

But your new responses now breathe the positivity, confidence and patience your children need to be successful.

Words Make the World

My early-career marketing company interview is the ideal example of how an adult or authority figure's words manage to maintain a strong impact—good or bad. Fortunately for me, my dad (and mom, of course) spoke life into me my whole life and though I left the interview hurt—for a short while—I quickly bounced back.

How? My father's words—the confidence, knowledge, courage and passion he had and imparted on to me. His words of life easily rose above the negativity that CEO threw at me. Not long after that dubiously fateful interview I got a job with another marketing company. I thrived in all sorts of creative and leadership positions. I was there for nearly 10 years before starting my own company that I still run to this day.

I took a negative dismissal on the chin and transformed it into a positive experience. But without the firm foundation of my father's loving and supportive words, his gift of time and teaching, and all of the cheering me on and believing in me when I was just a little boy, I couldn't have done that.

I might have let that CEO's negativity take me down without the words that were spoken to me growing up.

The light and joy and kindness and good behavior and confidence of your children reflects directly upon you and the light of love you shed on your children every single day—every single precious moment of time you have with them.

They notice what you say. They're wiser than we give them credit for sometimes. The positivity you teach your children will be like that ever-widening ripple in a pond. When your children are older, they will use the same language with their children and on and on and on!

Your words are everything. Think before you speak, and when you do speak, make sure you use every word to strengthen your children, help them love themselves, and help them know how very loved, how very precious, and how very much they truly are a treasure in this world.

Do You Want WHAT With That?

When I want to give my children a special treat and myself a firm reminder, I take them through the drive-thru and let them pick out their favorite fast-food meal, which invariably includes a chocolate shake for my son, a sundae for my daughters, and for me, a pleasant reminiscence. I place our order and think back to that CEO who shot me down so many years ago. I shake my head no and smile brightly when I hear the teenager ask, "Do you want fries with that?"

What My Son Said

My son: "Dad, can I call you bro?"

Age: 5

CHAPTER 8

We Were Legends

Every family holiday, my parents invite their brood back home to celebrate. First, it was just us kids—their kids—freshly out from under our childhood roof and on our own for the first time. But unlike earlier years, when it was just me and my siblings, the folks are hosts to even more company. These new guests are active, energetic, spirited, and amazing. They're our children—and they're just as excited to visit as we are.

Holidays are an especially good time for my parents to spoil their grandkids silly, overload their bellies and nerves full of sugar like some silent form of "payback," sending our children back home with us, sugar-inspired smiles brightly aglow on their adorable faces.

Dinner of course includes delicious food. But the star of the show? Stories. Always. There's so much to tell. So much we remember. And so much we love to revisit, because it's a special time. And because just being together—all of us—brings back our biggest and most memorable life moments. Funny. Embarrassing. Proud. Unforgettable.

The tales come so fast and furious sometimes—everyone rushing to get their words out as the memories become more and more vivid and inspired.

We take a winding trip down memory lane and avoid getting

dizzy by telling incredible stories of our funny, most embarrassing and memorable moments. But we all follow along. Because we know the stories by heart. They just seem to come to life so much more when we're all together.

The stories are infinite. We tell them in flurries. And while they fall and bounce around the room in a frenetic and joyful dance, I catch my dad as he stills himself, stares fixedly into the air, and prepares himself to share a memory or two of his own.

He's about to take it to a new level, basically.

Just before he begins to speak, the same thing happens that has always happened, and will likely always happen—as inevitably as the sun rises every morning and sets every evening.

He gives me the look.

The look that says he knows I know exactly what he's about to say. He ends his silent sentence with a raised eyebrow in my direction that also somehow speaks, saying, "don't you dare try to finish my sentence."

I respond silently in return, with a smirk, which of course, means, "Yep, I got it. Nothing outta me."

I've heard it all.

His first car. His crazy friends. The "walked uphill BOTH ways" trips to school. Blissful, summer days at the beach. The long, flowing hair of his youth. Smoking cigarettes under the school bleachers because it was "the cool thing to do." Replacing his car's seats with lawn chairs just because he could—it was easy to remove those seats back then. No matter how minor or outrageous the tale, he's told it.

He's knows he's probably told the stories many times. And he always looks at me because, again, he knows I know. Plus, I have a great memory. That figures into it, too.

My great memory, however, also allows for my very own childhood stories.

More or less, we've all lived a childhood just like my dad's. It may not have been on the shores of Daytona Beach or behind the wheel of a 1969 Pontiac Lemans but it did involve all kinds of unforgettable, life-changing, heroic, hilarious and hard-lessons-learned experiences.

As the saying goes: the more things change, the more they stay the same.

No matter the decade or even the varying external circumstances, childhoods, in essence, contain the same internal experiences—the lessons, the impressions, the disappointments, the thrills and the joys.

We want to share them with people we love—to reminisce, to laugh, to warn, to reveal, to remind, to bond, to let people into our life and, especially when we become parents, to teach lessons and offer direction, comfort and connection to our children.

Fatherhood Changes the Importance of Stories

Becoming a father is an amazing rite of passage in life, and one of its myriad rewards includes another rite of passage: giving your children a glimpse of who we were before we were dads.

And of course, we were legends.

Legends grow with the years, and the longer you live, the more legendary your tales of "back in the day" become. And often, those tales might already be just a wee bit "tall."

But that's just for fun. Tall tales and legends are great fun at family dinners. But embellished childhood—and especially the raw ones—are even more important when it comes to sharing them with your children.

Your childhood stories, unfiltered (or maybe a little filtered), are an incomparable passageway through which your children can get closer to you, understand you more, and learn very important truths about life as it is now and life as it will be in the future.

Introduce Your Children to Your Childhood

How? Stories. Just tell them your stories—about your mistakes, your successes, the fun you had, and the trouble you got into.

There are a few essential stories, however, that every son or daughter should hear about from their dad. (That's you, by the way.) They'll learn important lessons and find out about helpful guideposts from which to navigate their days.

But most importantly, they'll discover who you were before you were their dad. They'll find out about interests you may not have yet shared with them and that you may not even remember all that well until you start talking. Above all? Their connection with dad will grow even deeper. With every story.

What Your Children Should Know

Start with nostalgia:

Your Favorite Movies

(Real Life)

The Goonies, Space Balls, Big, Princess Bride, The Never Ending Story... the list of 80s movies I watched could go on and on. These movies weren't just movies; they shaped me and helped me believe in the power of fun, friendships, imagination—how to laugh. I forgot about everything and lived in another world created by, hey, a great story. I watched them over and over again. Maybe a million times. This isn't much of an exaggeration. They were depictions of my life. Well, except musicals. I. Stayed. Away. From. Musicals. Period.

(Learned Advice)

No matter what generation you're from, you've once connected with the John Wayne or Clint Eastwood or Mel Brooks of your time. Whether they were action-packed flicks, nail-biting thrillers, lip-locking romances, or slapstick comedies, movies were a part of you, and you surely watched several of them several times. These movies defined much of your childhood and inspired all kinds of emotions and dreams and beliefs. Share those feelings with your children.

The Music that Defined You

(Learned Advice)

Commercials, especially in the past five years or so, prominently feature music from past decades, dating far back into the jazz age to seventies rock to eighties pop all the way up to the nineties, early 2000s and even just a few years ago. Why? Music transports you instantly, right back to the moments you heard the songs. It's powerful, and brings out all kinds of tapped and untapped emotions, — connects you to what you and your life were like when you heard that song—once or many times over. And it definitely provides inspiration for ways to communicate with your kids about yourself and your past. It's so deep that your children feel it, too, and it inspires them to listen closely to you, your stories and to ask all kinds of questions—and to get to know you even better.

(Real Life)

What was my genre of choice you ask? Well, it was virtually everything. I listened to jazz, to rock, to contemporary-Christian, to rap, to punk rock, to everything else in between. I was that goofy white kid who pretended to be a rap artist on a

Monday (I wrote rap lyrics in my spare time) and used jazz as a way to focus during studying for a big test (and classical, too—I even did a little research on Mozart because I was impressed with his music). Oh, did I mention that I transformed my room into a studio with my brother, announcing the next "big hit" on our radio station WSCJW Talk Radio with your wacky host DJ Whiteboy. Music was the real deal growing up.

(Learned Advice)

Use the music you loved as a way to talk to your children about what they love now. Listen to music on your iPod together...or to keep the nostalgia alive, bust out a cassette tape. Don't forget to include the goofy things you did. Music inspires EVERYTHING. Especially goofiness. Don't regret it; own it.

Your First Car

(Real Life and Learned Advice)

I recently pulled out a picture of my first car. A mid-90s Camaro. Man, I loved that car. I showed my dad the picture and asked if he remembered it. Before I even got a response, he told me everything about his first car. The passions about our respective first cars bounced back and forth and overlapped. We were so excited to share about everything that comes along with a first car, including the car itself. Don't overlook the layered significance about conversations you have about cars...especially with your sons.

Move on to the memorable:

Your Big Achievements

(Real Life)

One of my most memorable achievements? A record I set, like a sports record. Ok, to be fair, my "record" will never see the record books. It probably will not be remembered by any person who was there to witness. But, I was. And I remember. Clearly.

I wanted to make the basketball team in seventh grade. I attended the tryouts. To be fair, I wasn't a good player. At least not at that age. The boys around me were better than me. They'd played on organized teams prior to tryouts. I only played pickup ball at recess. They were coordinated and knew the important plays you make in a real game. I knew to aim for the circular object when shooting the ball.

But, on this day, I would experience something I wouldn't see again in a game, ever.

The coach had us create teams of five boys for a scrimmage game. I was stuck with a bunch of guys I didn't know—we were the "rejects." I quickly introduced myself and jumped on the court with my team to start the four- minute scrimmage game.

In the first three minutes and thirty seconds, I nailed six three-point shots. I was unstoppable. It was a miracle, really. To top it off, as the clock winded while I dribbled the ball toward the half-court mark, a voice shouted, "shoot it!" The lock was at four seconds. Without a second thought, I heaved my tiny body—it was tiny back then, but now I'm towering at 6'3"—in a lunging position to throw the ball toward the rim. Somehow I fell toward the coaches' table positioned near the same half-court area. As I fell into their table, I heard the "swish" of the ball as it cleared through the net without even touching the rim. It was a perfect shot!

One of the coaches said, "Nice shot, son!"

Fortunately, I went on to make the school basketball team. Sadly, I scored only two points the entire season. But, during the tryouts—in that moment when the ball swooshed through the basket—I was a legend. At least in my own mind.

(Learned Advice)

Take a moment to boast about your successes. It will make your children stop in their tracks and think of their dad as a hero. Let them know what you've achieved. It's not simply boasting for boasting's sake or just to make you look good (though that always helps). It's good for your children to learn it's okay and actually very important to set goals, achieve them and be proud of themselves.

Start simple—like with the winning homework project that "wowed" your classmates. Move onto something bigger, like the school record you set on your baseball team.

Your "big achievement" can be anything. What's more important is how you make your children see it. As long as you build it up right, that guppy you caught in your kiddie pool when you were five *might* sound more impressive than becoming President of the United States. It's the way you tell the story that makes it "big." Your children will enjoy this. And hey, why not throw in actual "big achievements," if you like. Either way, your kids will love hearing it. And one day, they'll carry on your "tall tale" skills to their own children.

Your Favorite Vacation

(Real Life and Learned Advice)

Have you taken a road trip to the Grand Canyon in 120-degree heat? Or maybe you've experienced the winding roads of Napa Valley? How old was I when I had my most memorable one? And when I say memorable, I mean this vacation will go down as one of the goofiest trips I was a part of.

Jammed in the back of our family mini-van, I was packed in with the luggage since we didn't have enough room to fit. I'm sure my family contemplated hanging me from the storage rack on the top of the car (I was a moody teenager at times).

Our destination? Tennessee. A week-long trip packed with exploring, shopping (oh boy!), eating, entertainment...oh, the entertainment you ask? Well, this is why the trip was so legendary. We didn't go to big shows, but we did make a show of our own.

With our fancy 1989-style video camcorder (remember those?), my brother and I decided to take our trip to the next level. We turned an average trip into a documentary. The videographer: my brother. The host of the show: well, dads, that would be yours truly! The average trip transformed memories to a full-on feature-film complete with great (ok, slightly childish) humor, witty (I admit, corny jokes) banter, and insightful (yes, very clueless) information about the surrounding area.

This was THE vacation that I will never forget. And because of that, my children won't either.

Whatever trips you've taken, let your children know why the trip meant so much to you. They will soon plan their own trips and they will use the experiences you share with them as their own travel guide.

Your First Job

(Real Life)

Compared to some, my first job was a walk in the park—a local supermarket chain. My expertise? Bagging groceries. My most notable achievement? Mopping the floors to perfection. It may not have been pretty, but I remember it. All of it. To this day, when I go through the checkout line at my local store, I look to the person bagging my groceries and crack a smile.

Almost to say "I'm proud of you."

(Learned Advice)

Does anyone have a normal first job? OK, a few of you out there might, but for the most part, the nature of the two words "first" and "job" combine to equal all kinds of hilarity and, well, pain. When you tell your children about your first job, you'll surely evoke some long-forgotten memories you may really have wanted to forget for good...and, you'll certainly get some good laughs out of your children. (Hopefully your current job is less humorous these days.) From fast food to physical labor to being a house-sitter, your first job helped shape you. Some of those jobs led you to where you are today. Let them know why they were important.

Continue on to the unforgettable:

Your Biggest Screw-Ups

(Real Life and Learned Advice)

We have to admit that no matter how much we build up our past and how much we'd prefer to keep our past mistakes to ourselves, there are things we wish we had not done that we need to share with our children when the time is appropriate. I do not believe in burying the past. We can use every moment in our lives as a teaching moment. I don't encourage doing things that aren't right, but humans make mistakes, and it's crucial that you talk about the least-proud-of moments of your past so that your children can learn from them and not repeat them. A broken past can help build a strengthened future.

And because sharing this is so important, this one will stay between me and my children. Hey, some things in the family need to remain close to home!

The Relationship that Broke your Heart

(Real Life and Learned Advice)

Your children will fall in love and your children will lose

relationships and your children's hearts will break because of it.

My heart was broken. I was crushed. I felt defeated. And worst of all, I didn't think I would recover from it.

But I did.

I'll soon share with them how I got out of that heartbreak as a well and happy person. Not now, not even tomorrow. But at the right time, just when they are most vulnerable because of a broken heart, I will be there. For them.

They need to know they can lean on you when the time comes and learn from your own experiences, so that they can realize they're not alone. They need to know that an ended relationship is not their fault and that ended relationships are a natural part of life. And most importantly, that they have you as a dad to help them through it. When they see you smile, and that you are happy, and that you love them and love your life even though your heart was broken, too—when they see that you successfully came out of a breakup that broke your heart—it will give them hope and peace. Share your experience with them. It will save them so much suffering.

Finish up with the legends:

Your Funniest Moment

(Learned Advice)

You're hilarious. You know it. Your kids know it. Maybe you're not hilarious. That's okay. Either way, you've been bent double over on the floor with laughter quite a few times in your life. Share the best moments of side-splitting hilarity with your kids. Do your best comedy act and entertain them with the funniest moments of your life—most importantly your childhood. Choose a moment that has stuck in your head so concretely that you know without a doubt, it's the funniest thing you've ever been a part of. Share this with them and laugh while you're telling it to them. They may not laugh with you (let's face it, they most likely won't), but your happiness and your laughter— what they hear while you're telling that story—will stick in their memories. It will. So no matter what's happening in your lives at the moment, they'll forget it all and even if they're not laughing themselves, your joy will transport them, and all will be hilarity, even if it's only for a moment.

Funny? Listen to This

(Real Life)

I was about 7. My brother was 11. (Four years older than me. He was then. He is now. Go figure.) Anyway, we had this routine. You could call it a musical routine.

Well, sort of.

My dad frequently came out of his bedroom, his guitar in hand. That INSTANTLY queued us to run to our bedrooms and change into our "outfits." Stone-washed jeans pulled up way too high—way past our waistlines. This was intentional. We wore our long-sleeved shirts way too short—making them short-sleeved. Even though they weren't.

To top it off, the hat (pun intended). All neon. The brighter the better—perfect for the "show." At least we thought so, anyway.

With dad striking a tune with his guitar, our smiles aglow and our lips eager to sing, our little ditty went something like this:

> *"I was born on the backyard on a stump*
> *I was just a little tiny bum*
> *I was born with no hair...and no teefus*
> *and that's how I become...to know Jesus!"*

The routine was short, but we were AMAZING. The audience? My mom and sister. The act went triple platinum...in our house. And we were rich. Well, in our own memory bank.

In that moment, we were certified rock stars. And the hits just kept on coming...

Your First Relationship

(Real Life)

Her name was Allison. She was beautiful. She was kind. She liked me. I liked her. I felt like she really understood the real me. The things that interested me, she took an interest in herself. I even remember our talks. They were always so simple and sweet. We really didn't feel like we needed a lot of words. That's because we were pretty busy doing other things.

You know, like...swings, monkey bars, and slides on the

playground. Often an engrossing game of tag with our friends took up a whole lot of our free time.

We were in kindergarten.

But that didn't matter. I didn't realize that my age mattered. I didn't know what life ahead of me held, and how much more complicated and in-depth would all of it would be. I only understood who I was based on what I'd experienced in my short life. One thing I knew for sure, though. Allison was great.

We will always have our moment. Even if I was only in Kindergarten.

(Learned Advice)

You were probably pretty young when you had your first relationship. You will most likely embellish almost everything about this story. She'll be prettier, nicer, funnier, even famous, maybe. You may exaggerate a bit about how much she adored you. No matter how much you add to it and how much you leave out, tell the story. Everyone's first relationship was important—life-changing, actually, simply because it was FIRST. The details may be blurry, but no one forgets their first relationship. And by the time you choose to share this, your children will probably be old enough to date. So use this as a platform from which to dispel advice. It's a big deal. And it's best when it comes right from your heart to theirs.

Your Best Friend

(Real Life)

There are no words to fully describe my best friend. We met in seventh grade when we were paired up for a video project. Our subject: Sir Isaac Newton. The result? A three-day "video shoot" of us discussing gravity as if we were scientists ourselves. Back then, we rocked the puffy hair, the oversized glasses and colorful braces.

That project started a lifetime friendship.

Through the years, we shared every day together and were side-by-side through everything. The accumulation of those days and those "everything's" formed a legendary friendship. We grew up almost as one, forging legends with basketball championships at our local park, school projects that won every award in every category, double dates with the most beautiful girls in town, purchasing the fastest sports cars on the road, attending the best concerts in the state, and much, much, much more. All this, before we even graduated high school. True story there. Every word.

(Learned Advice)

Best friends are THE CHILDHOOD LEGEND. No experiences were more epic or more fun or unforgettable than those you forged with your best friend. When you begin, you probably will have a hard time stopping. So hold onto your plentiful reserve of wild chases through the woods (or the mall), movie nights, fights and make-ups and fights and make-ups, and especially how you met and how your best friendship came to be. Your children need to know about how friendships begin, change, how people change and how important a friend can be in your life—especially your childhood friends. After all, friendship is forever.

And, my friendship with my best friend will last forever.

Your List is Sure to be Different from Mine

But you have a list. Just make it. And share it with your children. Share your memories, your dreams, and your passions. And don't leave out the bad stuff. This is where they may learn their most important lessons. Chances are it's where you learned yours. Share it all as often as you like—you can stop before they know it by heart, but you certainly don't have to.

Past Perfect (Sharing the Past. Improving the Present.)

It was one of those perfect spring days—sunny, breezy and clear. My children and I were enjoying the day and the weather and decided to do a little "spring cleaning" on the garage. Before I knew it, I spied an umbrella. Minutes later, I was quickly searching for more umbrellas with my children.

We finally found enough to create a dome-style fort big enough for the three of us. Since it was a bright clear day, everything on the street was quite visible, and when cars drove past our house, people got an eyeful of awesome: our incredible round fort styled with all manner of colors, sizes and patterns of umbrellas. Like, the best igloo you'd ever seen. But even better, because it was bright and beautiful and also, in Florida. Those passers-by couldn't catch a glimpse of a person, just that bright, patchwork-patterned fort with the undeniable sounds of child glee—laughter, giggles, squeals—pouring from beneath.

I had the biggest smile on my face.

Why? Well, we were having a blast, of course. The umbrella led to this incredible idea, and we built the coolest fort of all time with the almost inexplicable number of umbrellas in that garage. I lost my adult self and all my worries as soon as I got the idea for the fort. I got to help them build this incredible thing, and the coolest thing about that? They took me right back to my childhood.

Without a warning, I was a kid again. I hadn't planned on that happening that spring day. But it did. And all of a sudden, as I watched my children build their fort and live their childhoods, mine came right back to me, completely unbidden.

It was a Saturday afternoon. But not the one I was enjoying with my kids. It was one nearly 25 years earlier.

In one hand, I held my umbrella handle, firmly grasping it to keep it from flying off with the wind. In my other, I held my favorite drink, sipping from it periodically. My neighborhood friend kept me company as we watched people pass the house.

It was a moment I hadn't thought of in years. A small, seemingly inconsequential moment, but it was real. A memory. My life. In it was contentment and pleasure. The kind of moment that children enjoy especially, since their lives so often reside only in the present, without future fears or past regrets.

Thanks to my children, that's how I felt then, watching them play while remembering a sweet day from my childhood. My gratitude for the memory and the present washed over me, and for the present especially, because my children were there.

Without the sight of my children playing with those umbrellas, that old memory likely wouldn't have revisited.

Our childhood stories are infinitely valuable. Their stories help our children navigate life, just as the stories of our parents guided us. My father tells me his childhood stories. I tell my children mine.

And in the telling, a window opens, and lets our memories loose.

"Wait. What year is it?"

What My Son Said

Me: "If you were in the woods all by yourself, what is the first thing you would need to do to prepare to go to sleep?"

My son: "Shut my eyes!"

Age: 6

CHAPTER 9

Life Navigation: A Survival Guide

One perfectly normal weeknight, after baths and brushed teeth and prayers at bedtime, I tucked my beautiful children in tight, kissed them goodnight, left their rooms a happy and content dad, then walked slowly down the hall with a smile on my face that said, "all is right with the world."

You know, playing the part of myself in a scene so perfect that it could only play out in a movie.

A little while after I left them snug in their beds—about the general length of time it takes them to truly and deeply "sack out," I decided to take a quick shower, preparing to kick back and relax for the rest of the evening.

After all, it had been a very long day.

They are almost always right on their way to dreamland just about as soon as their heads hit the pillow. Like most nights, right around this time, my children are sound asleep. We play hard. So they crash quickly.

A Knock at the Door

Just a few minutes into my shower, I heard a knock at my bedroom door. This was unusual for a couple of reasons. First of all, I'd left the door open. And my children never knock on my bedroom door when it's open. To be honest, they never really knock on the door when it's closed, either. They're welcome to come in as they please. And they know that.

I Began to Worry

But before the worry set in, my confusion, right at that moment, deepened. I mean, why would those two knock on my bedroom door when they never knocked? Ever. And why were they awake? Like I said, they "crash and burn" quickly, and sleep soundly through the night most every night.

Now I was really worried. I grabbed the first towel within reach and jumped out of the shower with an almost frenzied quickness. Dripping wet, I rushed out of my bathroom door to find my neighbor standing in my bedroom, along with my two very frightened children.

Said neighbor greeted me with a rather alarmed, embarrassed smile, doing her best to ignore my lack of shirt and shorts.

It was awkward.

But I had my own questions. Why was she in my house? And how did she get in?

My children stood next to her, crying their eyes out.

What was happening?

Frozen in my tracks, I was completely baffled. But my children were terrified, and immediately raced into my arms. I squeezed them tightly—acting as if I hadn't seen them for awhile.

"Are you alright?" I asked.

With their hands wiping away their streaming tears and their faces halfway buried into my shoulders, the two children whispered.

"Yes," they both nodded.

So What Happened?

It was a bit of a conundrum to me at first. From what I could surmise, the two had woken up and explored the house quickly, but they'd failed to check the bathroom, where I was. They couldn't find me. So they unlocked our front door and walked through the darkness to my neighbors' house, holding hands the whole way. They knocked on the door and asked for help, saying that they couldn't find me anywhere. Our neighbor listened and walked with them back to our house.

Why Weren't They "In Trouble?"

When I tell this story, people's faces give me the "I'm surprised you're not upset that your children left the house without asking you first" look. At this point, a huge smile spreads across my face.

My children had done EXACTLY what I taught them to do

when something scary happened at home:

- Leave the house immediately
- Head straight to specified neighbors' house
- Explain the situation and exactly what happened
- Tell neighbor exactly why they had appeared out of the blue

I made sure they understood that there was only one neighbor they were allowed to talk to in a case like this. I made sure they understood exactly where the house was and exactly who to speak to. And they'd done just that.

They Didn't Miss a Step

My son protected his little sister just like he was supposed to. He held her hand the whole time and made sure not to leave her behind. He kept her right by his side. They left the house from the exact agreed-upon location. Instead of going inside the neighbors' house, they brought the agreed-upon neighbor right back to our house.

My son then explained to the neighbor all of the steps he took to follow the plan I'd devised for this situation as they understood it—their missing parent. He filled our neighbor in on every single detail about what happened and what they had done to remedy the situation, exactly according to our plan.

He made sure our neighbor knew the full extent of what happened and why she had been asked to accompany him and his sister back to our house.

Our neighbor was in on the plan, too.

Textbook actions completed to the letter. Well, my textbook, anyway.

Taking Safety to the Next Level

I pray every day that my children will always be safe and secure. I pray that the children of every person I'm close to will always be safe and secure. I pray for the safety and security of all children.

But we dads need to prepare our children for the worst, and hope for the best.

To prepare for the worst and ensure the best possible safety and security for our children, we are not powerless. We can take every safety precaution available to us.

From alarms and locks on the doors of our cars and homes to all the mini-reminders and well-known precautions like orders to stay away from strangers, cross streets at the crosswalk, know their address and phone number, and know to walk on well-lit streets, we can take small steps to keep them as safe as we can.

But we can take it a step further.

In order to keep my children as safe as possible—most especially when they're on their own—I created a safety game plan for me and my children.

I encourage you to develop a safety game plan for your own family, too—a detailed play-by-play with no room for confusion or missteps.

Prepare for the Worst

Pray for Their Safety

Tell them that you pray every day for their safety and happiness. Tell them how much daddy loves them. Don't scare them, but make sure they understand how important it is for all of you to have a safety game plan you follow to the letter and memorize backwards and forwards, just like they would for a test at school.

Get Their Undivided Attention

Don't discuss this plan in vague, general terms. Don't bring it up as casual conversation while your children are half-asleep or only half-listening. Sit them down and ask for their full attention.

Keep It Simple

Once you get their attention, clarify the plan's importance—that it's been created to keep everyone safe, secure and prepared. This should be a very simple, clear, and direct plan clarifying what your children should do in case something were to happen to you and they do not see their parent.

Your Safety Game Plan—A Play-by-Play

Whether small children or older teenagers, your children may experience all kinds of frightening situations. What if they can't find you? What if they get lost? What if they witness or experience something traumatic? What if they've seen a crime?

These are real possibilities and you must discuss them with your children. They need to be prepared for the real world, and the real world can be dangerous.

Create A Plan

Identify the kinds of threats and frightening situations your child might face and create plans to get out of them safely. This list is sure to change over the years as your children face new life experiences. Develop a plan and outline clear steps that are easy for your children to understand and follow.

Communicate the Plan

If you don't communicate your plan, then it is not a family plan. It's just your plan, one that exists in your head. A plan can only be called a "family plan" if everyone in your family knows what it is, understands its purpose and knows how to properly execute the plan. Communicate clearly, slowly, and *frequently*.

Make a choice to discuss your plan with your children at the right time. When might that be? Preferably a time when: it's not dark outside, they're not currently recovering from a bad experience or when they're nodding off to sleep. You don't want to scare your children; you want them informed.

Have Them Communicate the Plan Back to You

After you have clearly communicated your plan in detail, have your children repeat it back to you. Help them complement their listening skills with their comprehension and verbal skills. When they repeat the plan back to you verbally, you'll know they'd been listening and you'll be sure they understand. Go over it with them again and again, and have them explain the plan back to you over and over again to be sure they understand completely.

The more often they repeat the plan back to you, the more confident they'll become with it and with what's expected of them. You want your children strongly equipped, not loosely prepared. This may seem tiresome to your children, but it will ultimately help them be prepared and know what to do if and when they need to put the plan into action.

Pray the Plan Never has to be Used

You've created this safety game plan for just that—your children's safety. You don't want them to have to put the plan to use, but the plan's purpose is to ensure that your children understand how to keep themselves safe should any frightening or dangerous event take place. It's a safety net in the face of reality. You will want to continually pray for the safety of your children and entire family. You do not want anything bad to happen to them. Pray for safety, protection and understanding.

And most importantly, pray your children will never have to put the plan to use.

The Safety Game Plan: A Strong Effect

Though I was at home when my children woke up and couldn't find me, it proved to me that the plan was necessary. If I never created such a plan for my children and made sure they understood it, they would have been lost. They wouldn't know who to talk to, how to get somewhere, or how to communicate to the right person that they needed help.

Whether or not it ever has to be used—and of course, we pray constantly that it doesn't, the plan possesses an important effect on your children's confidence and safety, as well as the sense of security and ability to help should any other people be part of the safety game plan.

Tighten Up the Plan with Simple Reminders

Time is of the Essence

In the case of an emergency, it's absolutely essential for your children to spring into action and carry out the plan immediately. Make sure they know that the longer they wait, the less effective the plan becomes. Actions bring about results—results like safety and escape. Delaying action and waiting for results can really hurt the plan and may cause undue stress and danger.

Creating Courage and Instilling Bravery

In a threatening situation, your children are going to be pretty scared. You're their protector, and you won't be there. Fear clouds logical thinking and can make it difficult to think clearly and follow through with the plan they know by heart. This is natural. When discussing the different scenarios that may come up, and the plan you've put into place to deal with it, fill their hearts and minds with courage. Tell them how much you believe in them. Tell them how brave they are. Speak about their courage and bravery constantly. Never stop telling them how fearless and strong they are. This will help prepare them for any situation. Dads, our words are powerful. And when we tell our children how strong and brave and courageous they are, they will begin to believe it. And once they believe it, their bravery and courage will be of a great benefit should they need it.

Mistakes Happen

Though your children have learned the safety game plan by heart and are doing their best to carry it out; though they realize that timing is crucial; and though they know in their hearts that they are brave in their father's eyes, mistakes still may happen. Teach your children that while the safety game plan is important, perfectly carrying out every detail of the plan isn't the point. It's about trying the best you can with what you remember. Mistakes will happen, and this is OK. It's just important that they do their very best to find a resolution and get to a place where they are safe. That's all that matters.

Carrying Out the Plan

So there I was in my bedroom, dripping wet from my cut-short shower, too distracted and concerned to dry off. And there were my children, a well of tears streaming down their tiny faces as they held onto me tight.

While they were scared and nervous, they were not weak or immobilized.

They knew the plan. And they carried it out.

I was very proud of how well my very young children handled the situation.

Though it was essentially a misunderstanding, given that I was in the house and they just happened to bypass my location, their actions proved that they took our planning seriously. When an adult (Dad) wasn't present (or so they thought), they sprang into action.

Though only five and six years old, my children behaved more bravely than some people twice their age.

My neighbor was impressed. She watched the conclusion of this short-lived dilemma unfold right before her eyes.

My children did the right thing.

With our second round of goodnights completed, I tucked them in extra tight and kissed them goodnight, finally ending the night safe and sound in their beds. I took a moment to pause and consider their beautiful, tender faces. I was even more happy and content than I had been earlier in the evening. Not only that, I was so proud of these small, amazing beings that my heart swelled.

Leaning against the doorway, I found myself in a reverie of relief, even though no real danger had presented itself. But now I knew that if something actually did happen to my children, they were prepared.

I left their rooms, finished my shower, dried off, and put on my own clothes for bed, ready, finally to relax.

Plan: complete.

CHAPTER 10

Lead. Greet. Converse. Smile. Don't Slouch. Say Goodbye.

We'd been in the car for *hours* once we finally pulled into my grandparents' driveway. And it was *late*, like, 10 o'clock at night, I thought. Honestly, I didn't and still don't know the actual time it was when we arrived. But the night had held its darkness for awhile. Which, to my almost-seven-year-old self, still with that vast and organic sense of time only small children know, translated simply to late. Which translated to 10 o'clock.

So, let's cut to the chase here and just say, for the sake of this story, we arrived at the magical home of my grandparents when it had been dark for awhile—at 10 o'clock at night. And we were finally there.

In adult time, the four-hour drive from our home to theirs was no big deal. But to me, it was an unbearable eternity. I felt like I'd lived a million lives by the time we got there. My family had just arrived at my grandparents' house nearly four hours away from our home.

"Are we there yet?" was my only question, a simple request, I thought, and quite reasonable given that it was taking FOREVER to "get there." The fact that I repeated it every five minutes was of no avail. I never knew when we'd "get there," until we finally, in fact, "got there." And my parents felt no relief until we got there.

But we managed nonetheless.

We parked. I could just see the main doorway, the rest of the home obscured by shadow. Two low-lit house lights glimmered into the night. This vision, burned now into my memory, held a certain mystery.

Every time we arrived, those lights amid the quiet of night welcomed us home, to my grandparents' house.

A Necessary Detour. The House

Before we go any further into this story, let's take a detour. Because I've got to tell you about this place. Technically and officially speaking, it was a house. It had walls and a roof and rooms and all the creature comforts that come with such a structure.

But this place is so much more than a house. It's a home. And a home lives inside the structure, built up by years filled with love and joy and growing and living and changing and family. And memories. And this one had a lot of memories. You could feel them. I think that's where the warmth—and the magic—came in.

My dad was only 10 when my grandparents moved in. Of course, to me, that could be a century, so long ago it was. My father was ancient after all. And my grandparents, older still.

This house was simply AMAZING. I loved that place. My

brother and sisters loved that place. And of course, my dad loved that place. The closer and closer we got to his childhood home. We could see it in his eyes and hear it in his voice. His body language changed. A weight lifted. He looked—free, like a kid.

You could tell that his whole childhood seemed to fill him up and lighten his mood. Its memories played before him—along with his childhood and the child that he was—a child who grew up in an amazing place. His aspect became calm and serene the whole time. An unbidden smile spread across his face when we were "almost there." He was just as excited as we were, and as we pulled into the driveway, he couldn't help but grin from ear to ear. I mean, c'mon, of course it did. This place was great. It was pure comfort. Pure respite. Pure magic.

To us, anyway. The kids. The grandkids. All of us.

It Was and Always Will be "Home."

Soothing sounds like sprinklers spattering water across the lawn were one of many comforting, familiar greetings. And the lawn was satisfying to look upon, its pristine condition a thing of wonder. The lawn was perfect. Gorgeous grass, each blade apparently the same length, spread flawlessly across the ground surrounding their home—almost a dictionary definition of the word perfect.

Just ask my dad and he'll tell you a story about that lawn. He and his dad made that front yard perfect; they planted tiny grass plugs into the ground instead of full pallets of sod. It took time. A lot of time. But it was worth it. Now, so many years later, that lawn still proves that their sweat and labor was worth it.

Seemingly endless and perfectly spaced oak trees, huge and proud, shaded that lawn, dappling light and shadows as the sun spun its orbit. The oaks, with their huge and rugged trunks, complete with rings of age knots, looked as though they'd been centuries in the making.

One more way to call this place home, so permanent it was, even in the front yard, those powerful oaks a testament to a home long-established and strong. It looked like security and safety— nothing that could ever be destroyed. It looked historic and inviting and it was so great.

Their one-story home's outdoor entryway felt like a courtyard, with short cinder block walls on either side, with two lamps glowing a dark orange light—a lovely light so different from those you find at most other homes welcoming you in from the night.

We haven't even gotten inside yet, and you're already in love with the place, aren't you? Stay with me. It gets even better. This courtyard held years of memories, documented lovingly with years and years of family photos, for this was where all important photos were staged. And there are a lot of them. A LOT. And, a lot of them.

Old family photos, whether on the walls or in albums, are yours for the viewing. And as a child they were a source of wonderment, and still are. Almost all of our family's photos were shot at that very spot, the same background showing the permanence of the home and that space while the photos testify the marching on of the years, plotting year by year the forward movement of time and change.

The 60s. The 70s. The 80s. The 90s. All permanently captured in front of that very courtyard. First, time marked the changing faces and growth of my dad and his sisters. Until all of those children had children of their own, and me and my brother and sisters and cousins became the focal point marking our growth and the passage of time.

House=AMAZING. Now, Back to My Original Story

I knew only a few steps would bring me through the front door, but the anticipation built rapidly nonetheless. Soon, I'd be passing through those courtyard walls and into the house.

Regardless of the time, the day, or the company inside, my grandmother always answered the door with the same warm, delighted smile with a greeting that says, "Welcome, welcome. Welcome home. I'm so glad you're here. And I've been waiting for you!" Each time the door swung open, every single time the door opened, she offered the same greeting. Each time the door swung open I felt so safe and happy and loved. And excited. It was a good feeling. And this time was no exception. Dad let me ring the doorbell—its orange light amazingly matching the lamp glow behind us, and there she was. Grandma. Welcoming us with that wonderful smile.

We'd arrived. We'd finally gotten "there." We were HERE. And I was so glad.

On this particular evening, as (FINALLY) walked through the

front door, around the entryway and into the main living area, I noticed there were more people there than I had anticipated.

See, even at the age of seven, I was very aware of my surroundings. "Men are visual." Isn't that the adage? And I was living proof. In less than a second, I quickly noticed there were people in the house who were unknown to me. Strangers. Who were these people? All my mind said and knew was, "I don't know these people and I don't like it."

I quickly scanned the room for a familiar face. I was determined to find someone I knew. Because you know what else I knew? The inevitable. My dad's jovial introductions. Of me. He'd start making his rounds, speaking sincerely and conversing briefly with each person. He is a polite, considerate man. Socially savvy, you could say. But his mingling was one of sincerity and welcome. He was comfortable and confident.

Though I could see the new people in the house—the ones I didn't know—I was still too shy to do anything but find a way to avoid them altogether. One person I knew from the top of my head to the tips of my toes, and he knew me just the same way. I scanned the room and found him. My grandpa!

"If I run straight over to my grandpa," I said to myself, "I will not have to speak to those strangers at all." I had this thing figured out and under control.

And just like that—in an instant—I found myself my next to him. I'd made it. Mission complete. Or so I thought. My victory didn't last long. I'd gotten in nothing but a smile before my dad called me away from grandpa, where it was safe, and over to him, where it was not.

This wasn't good. He had people with him. Strangers. I still feel the shyness and all of its attendant anxieties when I remember standing in front of these "strangers." I was overwhelmed with it.

To make matters worse, these "strangers" standing next to my dad were obviously waiting for ME to run over and stand by my father's side. I knew they wanted me to come talk to them. But, see, I did NOT want to talk to them. It wasn't gonna happen. Nope. No way, no how. I wanted out of there, and fast.

But as I made and my way over and checked my surroundings, I didn't see any escape in sight. I'd been observant but clearly not enough. At least not this time.

But. Here's the thing I didn't know, something my visual observations could never have detected. These people standing next to my dad weren't actual strangers—they were extended family. On my dad's side. But how was I supposed to know that? I didn't. But at that age, I don't think that would have made a difference in my desire to escape talking to them. I still didn't recognize them. Extended family or strangers, I still didn't recognize them which, to my extremely visually oriented little-boy mind, essentially made them strangers, anyway.

"It's so good to see you, Chris," my dad's cousin said. I stood there. My dad looked down at me.

"Shake his hand and tell him you are happy to see him, too," he said. This was not the action of my choice, but my dad told me to do it, so I nervously extended my hand forward in an effort to shake his hand. After all, my dad taught me to be obedient (check out the chapter about that subject, and you'll understand).

"My name is Eddie," he responded. We shook hands.

And that was it. It was over. It was done. In seconds, I was off in the other room playing with my own cousins for the rest of the night.

There was a (Hidden) Lesson

That night, in the midst my shyness and trepidation, the loud chatter of our family in a small room, and my dad's expansive excitement to see and spend time with his family, he unwittingly managed to teach me something important. Extremely important. Probably without fully knowing the impact it would have on me, my dad took a moment to teach me a life lesson.

Let's face it, I'm sure he did know exactly what he was doing.

He wasn't seeking an instant change in behavior; he was planting a seed designed to cultivate good manners, ones that would grow as I grew. He was planting (and planning) for the future me and my future behaviors.

He knew this was important; and he took the time to do this even though the house was bustling with all kinds of activity. With a lot going on around us, he still took the time and opportunity to teach me the importance of being polite and having good manners no matter what situation you may find yourself in.

Good manners are everything. And they can only be learned if they are taught. Just like my dad was teaching me right at that moment.

The Hard Knocks Guide to "Good" Manners

A child can learn good manners, or rather, what's inappropriate, from the school of hard knocks, otherwise known as the world at large, which doesn't design itself around your child's best interests. The results will often be painful for your child, and lead to begrudged "good" behavior, usually instilled from negative and painful and judgmental experiences. The manners may be somewhat appropriate, but if they are taught without gentleness and a watchful eye, manners will be more of a chore than a way of life. So. You could leave this lesson up to the outside world.

The Easier, Softer Guide to "Actual" Manners

Or your children can learn good manners and appropriate behavior from you, and every day offers up an opportunity to plant the seed and continue nurturing it. When you teach your children yourself, in your own way, and in the environment and situation of your choice, the power is in your hands—not the great big wide world's—and you can guide them with close attention and kindness. You can support them. Remind them. Gently correct them. And watch them as they grow.

Can you guess which route results in a better outcome for your child? I think you can. And the choice is yours.

Manners Matter

No matter what. No matter where you are or where you come from, one could easily say that manners make the man (and woman, OF COURSE!). They make life easier and they make you a better person. Bad manners are indiscriminate to socioeconomic class. No matter how rich or how poor, bad manners affect everyone. And so do good ones.

So Teach Your Children Well

Dads, it's important for you to teach your children manners in the most in key areas of their lives. From introductions to "new people" to behaving at school to ordering their own food at restaurants to everything else in between, these manners define how your children behave as they will help develop into (hopefully—that's up to you!) mature adults. These lessons are vital. You should NOT brush this stuff off.

Give Them a Leg Up in the World

Building manners builds confidence even if your children are naturally shy. Like when I was young. (You should see me now! I'm waaaaay better. And very confident, too.) If they're taught well, they'll be polite toward people they've never met before. And even more importantly, toward people they do know and interact with daily like you (the dad), their mom, and their siblings.

If They Don't Look Good, You Won't Look Good

Your children's manners are a direct reflection upon their

parents. They are. Good, bad, or in between. The more manners they display toward the world and people around them, the more evident it is that they were taught by thoughtful, considerate parents. And if children display the exact opposite of manners as far as the eye can see, generally speaking, they were never taught in the first place. Which, you know, doesn't speak so well for you as a parent. A dad.

So here's your chance to step up, dads!

All Manners—Large and Small—Are Important

Some people say certain customs are outdated, or that it's cute for a child to still behave like a toddler when they're actually in elementary school by this point. Everyone has an opinion. Manners are a reaction to just about everything in life. We could discuss this all day. Really. But I'm going to introduce you to my (opinions) list. And since we are making introductions, the one I will focus on involves, well, the introduction.

A Greeting. Teach Them How to Meet

Preface

That day at my grandparents' house, I felt shy and especially nervous. Without my dad's guidance and presence, I would never have introduced myself to those "strangers." There was no way I could have done it without him. However. Right by my side I felt the comfort of the one person in the world with whom I felt most safe and protected.

My Dad.

I might have managed to bypass the "greeting lesson" dad gave me that day at my grandparents' house. I'd done it before. When my parents weren't around, anyway. And I didn't even notice I was being impolite. I was shy and didn't want to bother. I didn't consider it inconsiderate. I didn't consider it important. Until my dad started teaching me.

Let's take my dad's greeting teaching game plan as a model. I'll teach you the greeting teaching method he taught me. Trust me, this is good.

A Proper Greeting

When your children visit family, meet your own friends, or get put in situations where they are introduced to new people, you should teach them how to greet them. Just like the old cliche goes, "you don't get a second chance at a first impression." The sooner you teach your children how to be polite and friendly when meeting new people, the better.

Your children need to get this much-essential part of the manners toolkit down. Now. They need to learn how to greet the people they meet in a welcoming, polite, and confident manner. Some children learn how to do this—because they are taught how to do this. Some don't—they weren't taught how. And it shows. Don't make that mistake. Teach your children this fundamental life lesson.

The Time is Always Now

At my grandparents' house, my father patiently navigated a frightening situation for me. But he knew this lesson had to happen, right then and there. So he helped me learn how to say hello to people, introduce myself, and greet them with polite consideration. From there, it became easier for me to greet people. With each new opportunity, I gained more and more of his confidence, knowing, too, that he had confidence in me. His consistent lesson, one he provide with every necessary introduction, made the action easier when he wasn't with me.

Approach

Make sure you have a face-to-face conversation with the person you're saying hello to. A brief nod of the head or a small wave across the room do not qualify.

This part of the lesson is for educating younger children. As you make your approach, ask them to walk over to the person with you. As they watch you, and stand beside you as you've asked, standing as you are at a close and polite distance from the person you want to greet—just by watching your body language, children will soon learn to act properly when you are not around.

Get Them Comfortable

Make it clear to your children that you are there to help them in this daunting process. Let them know you are with them every step of the way as they learn, situation by situation, the polite way to greet new people with confidence and warmth. When they're young ones, your presence gives them the security and confidence necessary for a proper greeting. They need you. It's now or never. This is the time. Start in on this lesson now.

The Lead-In

Because younger children are not familiar with leading a conversation, it's important for you to help them out here. Guide them through every single step necessary when it comes to taking the lead-in of a greeting. Give them simple, gentle nudges. "Say hello," "shake their hands," or "ask them how they are doing," are easy-to-understand actions and words for young children when they're learning how to begin a conversation with someone new.

Non-Sequitur Side-Note

Telling this story just reminds me of one of my grandpa's lead-ins. It's not exactly pertinent to this little guide, but it's not exactly off-the-mark, either, so please indulge me.

Whenever we arrived at his home during the day, it seemed he was always in the middle of a project, usually without his shirt and with a Carolina Gamecocks cap on his head.

Oh, yeah. And prescription sunglasses, dark and tiny with very thick frames (hipsters wear these now, by the way). As soon as he saw us walking up, he always looked up and said, "Hey, sports fan!"

Now. I did wonder what sport I was supposed to be a fan of, but soon learned that was just his charming way of saying, "hello!"

I've been a "sports fan" ever since. And I like that.

Okay. Back to what I Was Saying

Make the kind of language noted above as teaching points. They don't even need you to tell them that this is important. Trust me, your children are taking note.

I took note. In my brain, I could see myself jotting down the major bullet points:

The Lead-In, Simple Point by Simple Point

- I extend my hand.
- I provide a strong grip, displaying confidence.
- I make the motion of a handshake equal to that of the other person
- I make eye contact.
- I express myself with a facial gesture
- (This gesture should be a smile. No scowling!)

Your children need to get this list of actions down cold. Soon enough, it will be second nature for them.

The lead-in is just that. It leads into the rest of your conversation.

The Response

Once your children have the greeting down, teach them to wait for a response from the person they just addressed. Teach them greetings that require an open-ended response, which will warrant your children to listen and reciprocate. So expect your children talk for a moment here.

Questions are always great examples. Teach them to use them where appropriate. They'll have to answer questions, too. But that is easier. When a lull is looming, teach them how to keep the conversation going with open-ended questions like:

- "How is your family?"
- "What is something new you have done lately?"
- "Are you and your family doing anything interesting soon?"

Questions like these don't simply display good manners and extend the conversation, they'll show the person you're talking to that you have an interest in what they have to say.

Response is an absolutely essential part of this lesson. A response helps the person respond. Two responsive people = a conversation. A conversation?

Yes. Now We're Getting Somewhere

With my dad's help, I slowly learned that greeting people and talking with them wasn't a chore, and it wasn't very hard once you got the hang of it. Conversations allowed me to meet someone new, were something I could lead by asking questions and continue by answering questions—and I could talk about things that I was into.

Conversations can Actually be Fun(ny)!

Oh, and I could also inject humor—purposefully or otherwise. My responses were always entertaining. Once I got comfortable, I couldn't keep myself from making jokes during a conversation. (I guess that's where my son gets it from?).

Body Language

Smile and Nod

Body language communicates almost as much—and sometimes more than— words. The way that you stand. A firm handshake. Even the frequency of your smile. These unspoken forms of communication make conversations more pleasant. Teach your children to stand up tall, smile often, and nod their head responsively while someone is speaking. An active listener keeps the conversation going in a smooth, positive direction. Such body language shows that your children have good manners without them ever having to say a word.

Smile and Don't Slouch

My dad always taught me not to slouch. Stand up straight. Smiling and stopping isn't really smiling; it's impolite. Show people you're genuine (yes, he used big words to me like that when I was young. Remember when I said that children can only learn if they are taught? Yes, I meant it). He even taught me active listening. Just nod your head in agreement while someone is talking to you (you thought I came up with that on my own?).

Like (This) Father, Like (My) Son

As I started down this same conversation-education-people-don't-bite journey with my son, I felt like I was on the fast track. Sure, I taught him the same steps I was taught at his age. Be bold. Be polite. Introduce yourself. Smile and nod. Shake their hands. Respond. Ask questions. Respond again. So he was learning. Let's stop right here.

This One is Good

During this point of the conversation learning process, I was focusing specifically on how to greet people with hand gestures (no, it's not that bad!). Because I wasn't around new people too frequently, I chose to have him practice his greeting skills with my dad (his Grandpa, of course) whenever we went to his house. I was looking for the "proper" greeting we'd been working on. You know, stand up tall, extend the arm, provide a nice firm handshake.

We practiced this often enough. So after some time, I didn't have to remind him. The interactions were going great and my dad was impressed.

And Then There was This One Time

My son walked into my dad's house. My dad stayed on the couch, waiting for him to walk over and give his grandpa a handshake. My son extended his arm. My dad extended his. They grabbed each other's hand...and then my dad quickly pulled his hand away, falling backward in fits of laughter.

My son had folded one of his fingers in and instead of shaking his grandfather's hand, he just wiggled his own.

"That's my worm hand," my son said.

At least he knew to introduce himself without being asked.

And he definitely got a laugh.

The "Goodbye."

A long conversation isn't necessary for your children to display their good meet-and-greet manners or to prove their politeness capabilities. Simply providing someone with a brief moment of undivided attention indicates that they've learned strong communication skills.

And their "goodbye" can be simple, too. To start, just give them some simple "goodbye" statements like "It was great speaking to you," or "I look forward to talking more soon,." These are great phrases for a gracious exit that also lets the person know you're interested in continuing the conversation later.

Just like a book or a movie, a conversation needs a good beginning, a good middle, and a good end. No matter how well your conversation starts out, if it doesn't end well, you're going to leave a bad impression.

Teach your children that they should end their conversation EVEN BETTER than they began it. How? First, fill them in on the proper variations of goodbye. It all depends on where they are and who they're talking to. A handshake works just fine; it demonstrates a casual rapport as well as friendship. A hug for others is a must; it demonstrates care and closeness. And a kiss for a select few is essential; it demonstrates love, bond, and compassion.

Your children need to know the differences. No awkwardness necessary. But awkward moments are probable. Don't be concerned. That's just part of the process. The plan! But.

Sometimes it Doesn't Go According to Plan

Eventually, your children will learn to greet others with confidence, and they'll make you proud. You can smile, knowing that your lessons with them worked and that you taught them well.

And go easy on them when they fumble while they learn. Because they will certainly fumble. It's part of the process.

And It's Not Always Daisies and Roses

One day—a day far different than my successful meet-and-greet at my grandpa's house—my dad was about to introduce me to someone that I had never met before. A stranger. To me, anyway. I was still shy at the time. Very shy, to be honest. I was growing more confidence, albeit very slowly, so I anticipated the conversation I knew I was about to have.

I wanted to prove to my dad that I had this thing down. After all, he'd been teaching me the ropes for awhile. And now, I was ready.

Well. I thought I was ready.

I adjusted my stature and stood up straight. No slouching. I looked in the direction of the person I'd soon be speaking to, and waited for my dad to head in their direction. I was still tightly connected to the side of his leg. I was about 9 at the time and my hand clung to the side of his pants. The shyness was starting to overtake me.

But I refused to let it.

"No!" I thought to myself. I still remember my internal struggle. I was going to DO THIS. As we drew nearer to my target, I gallantly let go of my dad's pant leg and extended my arm in preparation for the greatest handshake of all time.

This was it! My moment!

MY time. I was the one. I was ready to step up and LEAD this conversation. And I did it!

"It's good to meet you, my name is Chris," I said with pleasant confidence.

"It's great to meet you, Chris," the soft spoken lady replied.

My dad leaned down, preparing for a whisper. "Son," he said, "I don't even know that lady!"

I'm sure my dad was both proud and amused.

It was a good try. Let's step up, teach them well, and be proud of our children in this process. Even if they do their best work with strangers.

As long as they're trying, they're on their way.

What My Son Said

Me: "Do you have a lot of poops or little poops?"

My son: "How should I know? I can't see inside myself. Besides, even if my eyeballs were turned inside out, it's still pretty dark in there!!"

Age: 7

.

CHAPTER 11

Number 1 (The Sleeper Hit)

You might think it's a little crazy, but I'm about to let you in on something that's a lot more personal than any of the other rather personal issues we've explored in this book. So I'm a little nervous to bring it up. But I will. With caution.

It's a secret. A big secret. An all-consuming secret. Or it was anyway, back when I was in elementary school.

We all have secrets, right? Imagine yours. One you're holding onto right now, or one you harbored a long, long time ago. Something so big that it's all you think about. Something you put all of your energy into hiding. That's what this one was like for me.

This secret was so big that it affected pretty much everything in my life. My whole world revolved around this secret, and in some ways—okay, most ways—I couldn't completely let go and behave and do the stuff I would have normally done, the things that I longed to do and WOULD do, if only this cloud of anxiety and fear didn't hang so heavily over my every waking moment.

It held the true me back. It held my life back. This secret was at the forefront of ALL my thoughts. And during these days, as the clock ticked its way toward the end of the day, I could hardly think of anything else at all.

The kicker? I dealt with all of this when I was young. Very young. Too young, really.

There was this time.

The school day wound down to its close, and as it did, all of the mounting excitement that had been welling in my heart and thrumming like butterflies in my stomach almost exploded (not in a gross way, guys, c'mon—it's a metaphor, or simile? I'm not sure. But let's move along.) This was excitement, not fear, so these were good feelings. Even though, thanks to this "good feeling," my stomach *did* hurt a little bit. But it was because I was pumped up. VERY pumped up. Maybe TOO pumped up. But anyway. The school day ended. Only one obstacle stood in my way.

The bus.

I leaped into my seat on the tenth row. I sat down with my backpack. I knew I wouldn't have to look at it for the next few days—I wouldn't be looking at *that* for the next couple of days. It was the weekend after all, and I wouldn't have to give that pesky thing attention again—not until Monday, anyway.

The familiar hum buzzed all around. Chatter. Jokes. The cool kids. The not-so cool kids. I looked out the window, not paying much attention to any of them. We were all headed to that familiar place. Home. And I. Could. Not. Wait.

IT WAS THE WEEKEND!

Finally, I was home! I ran through the door and up to my room, yelling "It's almost time!" to my mom as I whirled past her. She didn't stop me. Usually she would have told me to "mind my manners," with a proper hello. But my excitement had taken over by this point and she let it slide.

I was finally in my room. One step closer.

My room was cool back then. I shared it with my older brother. He was four years older than me and I wanted to be just like him. His toys and the things he was into...well, I wasn't quite old enough to be into those things yet. But I wanted to be.

On this day, however, it wasn't about his stuff. It was about mine. Specifically, the stuff going into my bag. An OVERNIGHT bag. Not my backpack. Remember. This was Friday. When I said I didn't think about that thing in the weekend, I meant it.

Shirt. *Check.*

Shorts. *Check.*

Hat. *Check.*

Socks. *Check.*

Underwea...oh no...wait wait wait! This was not good. This was not good at all. I mean. AT ALL!

A Secret Too Big for a Second-Grader

Excitement turned into fear. Fear turned into sheer panic.

I was FINALLY going to a sleepover with a friend of mine—a group of friends from my baseball team. I was finally invited. I was finally allowed to go.

There would be games. Baseball in the backyard. Food. I heard there was even going to be Kool-Aid there, too. Man, I was really hoping there would be Kool-Aid. I loved that stuff.

Wait. I paced. Wait, I thought again. No, wait! Wait. But I couldn't wait anymore. I had to think. I had to focus. I couldn't think of a lot of options. I needed help. I was only a second-grader, after all.

"Dad!" I yelled in one of my newly affected panicked-but-I'm-fine tones.

My dad came into my room with a look on his face that said he wanted to help but had no idea what was going on. It was a common expression.

"What am I going to do?" I asked him.

I didn't say anything else.

"What are you talking about?" he asked.

I didn't explain myself. I didn't give him any more information. I didn't really want to, either. I wanted him to guess, to just know. My secret.

I was invited to a friend's house for a sleepover. He knew this. I was getting my clothes together in preparation for said sleepover. He knew this, too.

He did not, however, know why I'd called him into my room.

There's one detail I left out of this story:

I wet the bed. Frequently.

I told my dad I was worried about the sleepover. I was nervous. Really nervous. I knew that I could get through the night without having an "accident."

But I was thirsty. Really thirsty. Thirst was my biggest enemy when it came to this particular problem.

I was thirsty and I knew my favorite drink in all the world— Kool-Aid—would be part of the festivities. A massive thirst plus the delicious satisfaction of an ice-cold glass of Kool-Aid combined? It terrified me. Would I be able to resist? And it didn't seem fair that I had to. I was just a kid, after all. And this secret caused me grief and struggle almost every day.

Oh, I loved Kool-Aid. Would I skip out on my favorite drink or would I drink it and potentially face the consequences? It was a very real problem for me. And I didn't know what to do.

This tension was constantly in the back of my mind—whether at home alone on a regular school night or with the added fear of someone spending the night with me and finding out about my embarrassing secret, leaving me fairly humiliated.

My dad knew the bane and burden I carried. He knew I tried not to wet the bed. I did try. My main solution was to drink little to no liquid in the hours before bedtime. I knew no other way. So this was my solution for the sleepover. But I was still so frightened and so anxious. My heart raced with fear.

My dad is a logical, sensible man. He kept the struggle as simple as possible and laid out my options, trying to keep it clear and sensible, and hopefully, a little comforting:

1. I could skip the sleepover
2. I could go to the sleepover

But I didn't want to skip it.

These opportunities didn't come my way often.

Plus, this wasn't just any sleepover. At least six or seven boys from my baseball team would be there: including the quick glove at second base, the "arm" that could throw any daring runner out from third. Practically the entire outfield, including our right fielder—who seemed to have two left feet.

Finally, my friend throwing the sleepover? He was the pitcher. A lefty. A good lefty. And he'd had a pretty impressive record that year. He was one of our most important players.

I was the catcher and I wasn't too shabby myself. I made the all-star team that year. I liked to think that it was because I could throw out players trying to steal second base or because no one could score due to my stellar home plate coverage.

My friend was the pitcher. I was the catcher. Almost our whole team would be there. The answer became a near-no-brainer.

I was going.

A Night Away from Home—Facing my Fear

With a push of the doorbell, the front door opened, revealing my friend, smiling hugely while yelling, "You're here!

Just like that I found myself in the backyard playing with my friends and having a complete blast. Few pleasures are greater that running around and playing games in the sunshine with your friends—especially when you're a child.

The party was just what I imagined it would be. Food, music, and...yep, Kool-Aid! My great love and my great nemesis wrapped up into one tempting and terrifying beverage. Unlike the Big Gulp you read about in this book—the drink that brought me great joy on so very many levels, Kool-Aid tortured me.

We had a passionate love/hate relationship during my bedwetting years. I loved it in the evening. I hated it in the morning. For obvious reasons.

But this time, I wasn't going to let the Kool-Aid win. I had devised a strategy to ensure that, tonight and tomorrow morning, I would be the victor, no matter how hard the battle.

And it was a pretty hard battle that day.

Outside in the backyard, with most of our team there, we played a baseball game for the record books. Of course, it wasn't official. But we played it just like we did our regular games—exerting tenacious concentration and furious play right to the finish. When the game was over, we were all winded, wound up, and thirsty.

Once the game was over, my friend enthusiastically offered me an ice-cold cup of Kool-Aid.

There was no way I could shy away. So I took the drink. I held the cool plastic cup in my hands—filled as it was with the most magical beverage I knew, second only to the Big Gulp, of course. Though my throat was parched and I was so very thirsty, I held that full cup for what seemed like an eternity, then dared only the tiniest of sips.

I was in the midst of a great and challenging battle. My thirst versus the dangerous consequences that would follow if I were to succumb to quenching that great thirst.

I think I had two or three sips the entire evening, holding onto the barely touched cup throughout dinner and the rest of the evening, all the way up to the hour when the pitcher's dad—our team coach—rounded us up to wind down for the night and get ready for bed.

"Bed?" I couldn't go to bed.

I quickly scanned my surroundings—this was one line of defense, my quick ability to rapidly take note of everything within my line of vision. I was an exceptionally visual child, as I've mentioned before. And in situations such as this, the talent was definitely my ally.

I scanned the room, looking for one particular item, in such a stealthy and discreet manner that no one noticed, thank goodness. Even this innocuous act, in my hypersensitive state, could NOT be noticed. I kept all signs of my rising anxiety at bay, lest someone discover my dreadful secret.

They were on the verge of figuring out my secret, I just knew it. When you're a child, you don't really quite understand that people pay much less attention to you than you thought. I was sure they noticed every telltale sign of my strange behavior. Of course they noticed my clinched almost-full plastic cup of Kool-Aid, the one I'd been carrying around all evening, almost like a safety blanket.

Why was I still carrying this thing? Even the cup scared me. And the delicious nemesis inside terrified me. I had to get rid of it. How could I do this without attracting attention and suspicion?

Finally, I decided to sneak my way into the kitchen to get rid of the Kool-Aid. It was evidence, after all. Evidence of the terrible act that had yet to happen. I had to get rid of it. Fast.

I found the sink and quickly poured the Kool-Aid down the drain, looking carefully over my shoulder, frightened that I might get caught. And while Kool-Aid was my enemy, I still remember bidding it a wistful farewell, as the contents washed down the drain. "I'll miss you ole' buddy," I thought to myself.

The drink was finally gone, but the night wasn't over. At least not yet. But I was making progress.

When I left the scene of the crime (killing that close frenemy, Mr. Kool-Aid, quickly down the pipe of doom), I noticed all of my friends had left the family room where they heard the "hey, it's bedtime" pep talk from coach.

There was noise coming from the back room where everyone was midway through putting on pajamas, big shirts, or some chose to only wear shorts with no shirts to bed.

This variety of chosen sleeping attire was a good thing, a very, very good thing (see, there are so many steps to keep this secret at bay!). Thanks to the shirts and shorts and only shorts guys, changing into my backup clothes would be no biggie.

If I had an accident I could carefully, quietly, and cautiously sneak into the bathroom, change my clothes and make it back to bed undetected. Then, if they suspected anything, I could let them know that I was hot and had to change into something cooler.

Yeah, that would work. It would work perfectly. Maybe. Ahhh, I didn't know if it would work! My internal debate and gnawing anxiety just grew stronger and stronger now that the acid test (bedtime) had finally arrived. The fear practically had a chokehold on me, even though no one around me knew it.

Just as I was feeling at least a little okay thanks to a semblance of a plan, that small glimmer of something like peace of mind was blown to smithereens. It was one of the worst possible scenarios for a bedwetter at a sleepover.

"You've got the top bunk!"

"Who? Me?" I said to the pitcher.

"Yes, of course! Who else would I offer it to?"

Of course he offered me, the catcher, what he considered the prime sleepover spot.

We had this special pitcher-catcher bond thing going on all season.

I could easily read what pitch he wanted to throw next. Mostly it was a fastball, so I would point my index finger downward behind a batter in a game signifying that I wanted the heat. Occasionally I knew he wanted to throw something different.

That's when the curveball came into play.

That's exactly what I was experiencing, only this time he was throwing ME the curveball. But if I took that top bunk, all of my careful planning would be for naught. And I might get caught.

My Dad came up with half of what we both considered to be an almost foolproof escape plan in case the worst happened.

See, Dad was my resident expert on this subject. He was no stranger to numerous contingency plans for eluding the notice of friends and adults when it came to the issue of "accidents" during his own perilous childhood career as a bedwetter.

The other half of the game plan was all me. The tip toeing. The extra change of clothes. The "I was hot and had to change my clothes" story.

This top bunk thing would ruin the WHOLE PLAN.

"Sure man, thanks!" I said.

Thanks? Why did I SAY that? I had an out! I had at least 3 other outs for this: the three guys standing next to me. If I'd said no, one of them would have taken the bunk. And I would have been safe for the night.

But I blew it. I struck out.

There I was, laying on the top bunk, a small glimmer of light coming in from the living room. I had my eye on my backpack, my extra set of clothes poking halfway out of the bag, carefully positioned by the door. A direct line of sight to the bathroom. I knew what I had to do if I had this accident. It would just be trickier to pull off now.

After the chatter from the boys settled down over the next hour, I found myself laying there in silence, completely exhausted and completely wide awake.

Those minutes on the top bunk felt like hours, and the hours felt like a lifetime as I stared at the ceiling thinking and worrying and thinking and worrying.

Just as yet another worry faded slowly across my consciousness...

"CHRIS, get up!!!"

Startled, I jumped wide awake, stock still, sitting straight up in THE TOP BUNK. It was morning. MORNING. I didn't mean to actually sleep.

And just like bedwetters everywhere, my immediate thoughts upon waking turned straight to anxiety-ridden damage control. And fear. And talking to myself, in my head, of course.

I didn't get up in the middle of the night. *Or did I?* I didn't remember.

I was so tired.

I remembered my clothes. My clothes. They weren't where I left them. *Where were they?* I looked down. I was wearing the same shirt I wore to bed. I paused. I wasn't yet sure if I'd wet the bed.

I was so used to feeling this worry and confusion every morning—right when I woke up—I couldn't tell the difference anymore.

I couldn't bear to look. This could be the single worst situation I would face. In. My. Life.

I lifted my shirt and took a peek. It didn't look wet down there. I carefully reached down and touched the mattress.

"Yesssssssss!!!" I yelled out.

"What are you so happy about?" the pitcher said.

"Oh...nothing!" I said, hurling back the phrase faster than his normal fastball.

I'd escaped. I'd won! I didn't wet the bed!

VICTORY!

The Sleepover Effect

What I experienced during my sleepover was both good and bad. Mostly good, but we'll cover the bad as well.

First Things First. The GOOD Stuff

I had a blast at the sleepover. All kinds of great stuff happened, right? We played like madmen outside, a masterful baseball game, running around and laughing under the shining sun. We had unlimited access to all kinds of the favorite foods children crave but never get to have all that often. And of course, I got to enjoy it all with a ton of friends, guys I was especially close to. My baseball team! This was the good stuff.

The Not-So-Good (Bad) Stuff

In the midst of all the fun, my secret was always lurking, undercutting what was supposed to be a completely carefree time. With the secret came all kinds of worries and thoughts and plans that I had to keep from everyone around me, no matter what. I had to be on guard at all times.

This was the bad stuff.

For me, all this bad stuff—all the unfun and worrisome and scary things I had to do or plan made one of the best sleepovers one of the worst, too.

Remember, this problem bedwetters have is a big secret, and what kids with my problem need to do to keep the secret, a secret, must be a covert mission and there's no rest until that mission is complete.

I've come up with a name for all the bad things that happen to us kids who wet the bed. The Sleepover Effect.

This effect isn't always in effect, meaning that children only experience this during certain times—mainly those times when you CAN'T have an accident. This could be during a sleepover. Spending the night with family members unaware of your nightly trial. Or when you have your own sleepover at your own house—in your safe zone.

So. What are the effects bedwetters experience in such vulnerable times?

Sleep happens. Rarely

Every sleepover. And I mean every single sleepover, you are getting the least amount of sleep. Because the longer you're awake, the less likely you are to have an "accident." Even when you're exhausted. Thanks to the ever-present anxiety, you're probably the MOST EXHAUSTED child in the room. Or house. Because on top of the normal physical exhaustion that comes from a big day of fun and play, you've spent all of your mental and nervous energy worrying about what might happen. And once you're in bed, your mind won't let you sleep. The constant fear of what might happen if you fall asleep keeps you wide awake until your body and mind finally give in to sleep. You can't hold it off forever. It has a mind of its own.

Sleep becomes your worst enemy, especially when you really need sleep, want sleep, and are so very, very tired. Your thoughts start blurring as you continue the spiral of overthinking and overcomplicating the situation you're in. And to a child, it's definitely a "situation." A potentially MAJOR situation.

Thirst. You're Always Thirsty

Even though you know there is adequate time to use the restroom, you fear that drinking anything remotely close to a liquid could reap some terrible consequences. And because of the gravity of the situation, those consequences could mean big time humiliation. So to prevent this, you start cutting back on the liquids. The later it gets, the less you drink, and because you are exerting more energy than normal while you're having fun with your friends, your thirst increases at a rate your brain tells you is unbearable. And yes, for those who've never experienced this, it's torturous.

Your Bed. It's Kind of a Big Deal

To most kids, a bed is a place to sleep. For children who deal with "accidents," that bed can be your saving grace. For a few key reasons. The proximity of the bed to the bathroom. The amount of people between your bed and the bathroom. Whether or not you can sneak from your bed to the bathroom undetected.

But then there is the actual bed. How are the sheets? Are they thick? Light colored or dark? Would they be hard to take off if you needed to? These things sound silly to others, but it's of ultimate importance to you, the bedwetter. They're serious factors. And always at the top of your mind.

Clothes. They're a Pretty Big Deal, Too

For the less worried children, the ones without this gnawing secret, bedtime apparel options are practically endless. But not so much for the accidental bedwetter. For instance, thickness is a key factor. Thicker clothes are more absorbent. And even though you're way too young to have to be thinking about such things, you have to. This helps you keep your secret. Somewhat. So you try to pad your clothes the best you can. Sometimes you even take off your shirt no matter how cold you might be—

because that means you won't have to deal with yet another item of clothing should anything go awry in the night.

The Sleepover Do Over

I knew there would be a solution for that lifelong thorn in my side—that secret that had plagued me all of my life—and while it may not have been a long life just yet, it was mine, and it was all I had to go on.

Nonetheless, the solution came. I thought my bedwetting days were behind me. And they were. My own bedwetting days, anyway.

Fast forward to me and my own offspring. My boy. I have a son nearly the same age as me in this story. He had the same challenge I had. He was a bedwetter. Of course, he can thank me for that. Just like I can thank my own dad. We can all, apparently, thank genetics. It's a generational legacy, apparently. Thank you, ancestors.

I want him to be equipped. I want him to be prepared. Confident. I want him to understand himself well, to know what to do no matter what the situation.

Soon, he will be invited to a sleepover. And he will be ready. I'll make sure of it.

From a dad like myself who found himself in such situations more often than not, I've devised a list of challenges and subsequent solutions for every sleepover hurdle the bedwetter must face. He'll be ready to conquer any sleepover he may face.

Every. Single. One. Ever.

Prepare with Proper Packing

It starts with preparation. If you were a bedwetter like me, you will know that having the proper clothes is essential. Why have one backup night outfit when you can have two? Why have two when you can have a third? Overboard doesn't play into preparation. The more, the better. Better is always best.

Pack your night time outfits in groups. If your children wear just a shirt and underwear to bed, put those two items together. Don't pack shirts together and underwear together. That means in the middle of the night, they will have to fumble longer through their clothes to find what they need.

When I was laying there in that top bunk at my friend's house, I stared at my backpack positioned perfectly by the door. I knew every order of everything in that bag. I was ready for it.

My son will be too.

Play Hard. Pee More.

Your children are at a sleepover. They will be busy with video games, outdoor games, board games, any kind of game that you can think of. Their mind will be in overdrive with excitement. But they must keep a mental clock ticking and enforce a personal rule to hit the bathroom every hour on the hour before they fall asleep.

For me, my dad helped me out with a game plan. First, he made sure I was prepared to go. Before I went to any of my friends' houses for a sleepover, he asked me if I was ready. I said, "yes." He asked me again if I was ready. I said "yes," again. He then asked me if I was ready. I said, "Dad, yes, I'm ready!"

He told me I needed to remind myself to be ready for bedtime the whole night. His persistent line of questioning if I was ready put me in the preparation mindset and served as a reminder for me to ask myself the same question all night, every hour, throughout the whole evening, to consistently ask myself, all evening, if I was ready—all the way up to bedtime.

His lesson? Play hard. Have fun. But remind yourself to hit the bathroom. And often.

This was an important lesson. And if I followed through with this good advice, I wouldn't have a problem.

Go Light on the Drinks

Why drink a full glass of water when a half a cup will do? Pay close and persistent attention to how much liquid you consume during the evening. Don't lose count, but don't get thirsty either—that only makes the later hours of the evening worse. Quench your thirst minimally and moderately, and NOT ALL AT ONCE. The old saying that "it's a marathon, not a sprint," holds true when it comes to securing a great night's sleep without wetting the bed.

Don't be afraid to turn down a drink. It's okay to decline. Also, learn to have a cut off time before bed. An hour before bedtime is ideal. Anything after the cutoff must be limited to a sip.

Gulps are bad, sips are perfect.

Don't Psych Yourself Out!

Focus on having fun. Pay attention to your good times and don't let your mind stray into worrying so much about whether or not you're going to have an accident. Worrying doesn't help anything and it keeps you from expending an exhausting amount of mental energy—energy meant for fun with your friends! Just be prepared. Know you're prepared and JUST HAVE FUN with the consoling and certain knowledge that you have a plan. Keep your eyes set on the preparation you've already devised and are putting into play throughout your evening. Go to the bathroom every hour, consistently. Be sure you do these things. Remind yourself. Follow the plan. And remember, remind yourself every hour of what you need to do. That's all. Know you have a plan. Follow the plan.

But whatever you do. Don't psych yourself out with useless worry and analysis.

The Dry Truth

My son is going to be prepared. He is going to understand how to go into any sleepover with confidence and security, knowing he has a plan, thereby losing all that awful worry that so easily latches onto the thoughts of children who wet the bed.

This is the strategy my father taught me. This is the practice my father followed himself. It worked for both of us until we passed that stressful phase.

Hey, we may not want to admit it but if you've ever wet the bed before, you know that it's not an easy thing for children to have to deal with.

But with planning, motivation, some cheering, a lot of compassion, a lot of reminding to remind themselves of their game plan, and careful guidance from a role model (dad) who knows all about the motivation, and great guidance from a Great that knows and has intimate knowledge of the situation their child is about to face, they'll be in great shape.

And dry.

A Conversation with My Son

From reading this book, you probably have a pretty good understanding of the type of dad I am. I'm pretty straightforward and LOVE to have straightforward conversations with my children when the time is right. The collaboration and discussion helps not only your child, but you too.

We're often in the car, too, as you also may have noticed. And a lot of major lessons are learned on both sides in this very common setting—driving from here to there all over town. And on this day, as on many days, there was a relevant and real-life funny story about to take place (you can pretty much count on my son for funny conversations). It was brewing right in the car as we drove along, and I had no idea it was coming.

And it's completely relevant to this chapter.

We were headed to a friend's house. The kids were pumped, thusly, LOUD. C'mon, they're children. For kids, building energy and excitement equals loudness. Plus, they get this from me. I'm ALWAYS loud when I'm excited. Again, genetics.

I noticed that my son started to get a little quiet. And if you knew my son, you would know that quiet usually equates to some kind of trouble. This day proved no exception.

"Is everything okay?" I asked

"Dad, I have to go to the bathroom!" he said. Loudly.

I asked the typical dad follow-up question.

"Number one or two?"

Without hesitation, I heard a "TWO!"

Knowing he meant business (and needed to do his business), I said "Ok, we are rushing to stop somewhere!"

I'll never forget what my son said next.

"Dad, now it's worse. It's gone to a number 8!!"

At least he's ready to tell me when he's ready.

What My Son Said

My son: "Hey, there's a slushie!"

Me: "Where?"

My son: "Look...6 o'clock!"

Age: 6

CHAPTER 12

The Big Gulp

"Let's go!", my grandfather, more commonly known in our Lebanese-American family as Gido (pronounced ji-doh) said. Gido spoke in a stage-whisper, loud enough only for my little ears. He clandestinely uttered this mock-conspiratorial command for me and me alone. Just the two of us. In on a secret. He made sure no one else heard. We snuck out of the house undetected.

I looked down at my feet to make sure my shoes were tied tight enough for the adventure ahead, then bolted out the door right behind him, racing with a racing heart, and finally bouncing into the front seat of my grandfather's car.

Though still very young, I already knew the routine. It always started out just the same--sometimes with an urgent shout ordering me to get a move on, sometimes a sly whisper in the ear, sometimes even a nonchalant "let's do this" glance from across the room, sometimes with a discreet tap on the shoulder--but it always ended the same.

Gido and I sat side-by-side in the front seat. I remember everything about that car. A solid white two-door with purple trim. And this wasn't just any two-door. These doors were heavy steel. I mean HEAVY. So heavy that I did my best to hide the severe physical effort it took me just to get them open AND shut. See, I was a big boy now, and able to handle such things.

These familiar steel doors were no big deal anymore. Once those doors were shut, the Bonnie-and-Clyde-spirited mission began. I sunk deeply into those plush seats, diminishing my already-small stature just that much more as I sat in the passenger seat and looked out of the window. Not soon after the drive began, sweat trickled down my brow.

Even with the windows open, that car held heat better than the Sahara desert. Which would have been nice in winter, winter in New York, maybe, but we were in the sunny sub-tropics of Southern Florida.

Gido stuck the key into the ignition, sparked the engine, and backed out of the driveway, the house behind us. We'd escaped!

Sitting next to him in the car, I'd ask where we might me going, pretending I didn't know.

As we drove, he'd make a side-glance at me with a half-smile on his face, a twinkle in his eye, and say--his smile wide now as he looked ahead--"You'll like it when you get there." The smile-lines around his eyes crinkled more deeply as his he drove with amusement and joy toward our destination. He thought he had me.

But of course, children are precocious, and know a whole lot more about what's going on than we give them credit for. They also know how to keep a good thing going. So I never let on. I'm glad I never did. These secret trips were one of his life's greatest joys.

The big adventure took fewer than five minutes. I did the famous run-walk across the grease-and-fuel laden concrete and practically vibrated with excitement when I reached the destination.

I paced quickly, back and forth, along the parking lot's adjacent sidewalk. Looking up, the majestic sign emblazoned at the building's entrance. It never failed to transform any of my expressions into a thrilled and beatific smile.

We weren't at the gates of Disney World, or even at the movies (though that would be the next best thing). We were at the greatest place. Like, EVER.

We Were at 7-Eleven

7-Eleven? That's right, the thrill of a lifetime (OK, maybe in that moment). We'd reached the magical place I always hoped to reach every time we set out on our secret adventures. I rushed through the parking lot to avoid the gasoline car exhaust fumes wafting through the air as adults poured in and out of the parking lot for a quick refill. But it didn't matter. Adrenaline pumped through my veins. We were here.

And it only got better.

Seven seconds after I'd leapt from my grandfather's front seat, there I was, standing at the store's entryway, which just so happened to be semi-hidden behind my waiting grandfather. As young gun, I was always pretty shy, so I hid a bit from his sight.

Of course, I was also playing coy, not really revealing that I knew why we were there.

He never let on about the mission at hand, just stood looking at me with a straight, practiced poker face. Oh, he thought he was crafty. Really, really crafty, actually.

He brought me here for a surprise. And kept his act up well.

"Ok, listen up," Gido said, pointing his index finger for emphasis. Whether playful or serious or seriously playful, Gido always used that finger of his to make sure you knew the deal. And here's the thing—the stuff of Gido legend, and a source of wonder for his grandchildren—that finger, thanks to a long-ago accident, didn't bend. This beloved idiosyncrasy of his just made us love him that much more.

"You have two options here, and I'm only going to say this once!"

Right about now is when I looked at him with innocence, playing right into the role of a clueless child. Hey, I had to play my part, too.

"Ok, what are my options?" I said in a boyish, puzzled voice.

 "You have your choice of *one* of two things" he said. "You can either have a candy bar *or* a Big Gulp."

Then the dilemma set in. A pretty serious one. I had one choice.

On one hand, the vast, colorful selection of candy bars lining the best aisle in the store was almost too much to contemplate.

Almonds, caramel, marshmallows. All of these options and more filled the center of a delicious chocolate bar I could wolf down—with glee!—on the ride back home. I could get creative and go for a Twix. This would give me two bars for the price of one. The possibilities of intoxicating chocolate deliciousness was practically endless.

On the other hand, however, there was the Big Gulp. This was something I could make last. I could savor the cold refreshment of a Big Gulp. Has there ever been a name so perfectly fitting? The legendary Big Gulp was so huge that a little guy like me couldn't possibly finish it. But, oh, I could dream.

The mighty Big Gulp—almost mystical in those neon 7-Eleven lights—beckoned brightly. The Big Gulp was massive, ice-cold, and I could fill that cup with perfectly cubed ice, topping it off with just about any soda flavor imaginable—lemon-lime, cola, orange, grape, cherry, root beer, ANYTHING—and that refreshing deliciousness would LAST...for a while!

I always took this important decision very seriously. Thoughtfully weighed the myriad pros and cons. And no matter how many times I'd been faced with that very same decision (let's just say it was rather often), the final answer was always the same.

Now. Let's step back a minute, take a break, and let me fill you on this story's undercurrent.

It's pretty special. Almost as special as the Big Gulp itself.

My grandfather always took me on these impromptu 7-Eleven missions at the most unexpected moments, making the getaway part was as big as the prize itself...usually close to dinner time during big family get-togethers, or just about any time when we just probably shouldn't have been doing any such thing that might "ruin our appetite" for whatever good stuff was getting cooked up in the kitchen.

"Don't tell Grandma!" he'd warn, this phrase itself the stuff of sweet familial legend. He didn't say this to keep Grandma out of the loop. This was just a way to give me the sense that we were in on a special secret—just the two of us. And children, especially when enjoying that exciting chance to be in on what we thought no-one else knew about, just added to the thrill. And put a big smile on our faces. It had nothing to do with us "getting away with something." Of course, Grandma knew what our Gido was up to. But we children were none the wiser.

And that's why he made sure to say—on this and so many other occasions too many to even name, "Don't tell Grandma!"

It always put a wide smile on all of our faces. And it still does.

His mission that day was to do something that was just for me and for me alone—something unexpected and surprising and therefore, a way to let me know how special I was to him, making our fun together that much more important. He was focused on that—SHOWING me how important his grandson was to him. He had a talent for that. I always made sure to thank him profusely. "Gido knows!" he always said. And that was true in more ways than one.

"I'll take the Big Gulp," I said to my Gido just a few quick seconds after an intense internal debate about my options.

"Why did you choose the Big Gulp instead of the candy bar?" he always asked.

"Simple," I said. "If I get the candy bar, I'll get thirsty and want to wash it down with a drink. The whole time I'm eating that candy bar, I'll be thinking about that. But if I get the Big Gulp, I can drink without feeling like something's missing."

"You've thought this through," he said seriously.

I smiled.

We walked to the bright Big Gulp drink machine and picked out the flavor. Surveying the long row of flavors overjoyed me with a vast sense of possibility and excitement. When I finally made my choice, the Big Gulp cup filled to the brim, I had to use both of my small hands, wrapped tightly around the glistening cup, to grab it off the counter.

Once I held the Big Gulp in my hands, enjoying the sweet refreshment as we made our way home, I remembered to thank him and tell him how much I loved the treat.

"Gido knows!" he'd say, smiling big as he drove us home.

This was childhood joy in its purest form.

In the world I grew up in, the Big Gulp came to symbolize the simple act of doing something special for someone you care about.

Wanna do the same thing in your family? Let me introduce you to how you can fill up your own life with just such a simple, powerful way to help your loved ones—especially those kids—feel as important my Gido made me feel.

Get Your Own Big Gulp

No, I'm not trying to be rude and tell you we can't share a drink (I have another chapter somewhere about sharing). But I do recommend you find your own special Big Gulp-style adventure to share with your children—one so memorable and important to them that they'll naturally pass it down to their own children.

First of all, your approach is almost the most important part—it's the bit that will turn your personal Big Gulp trip into tradition. Without a skilled approach, it'll just be a soft drink, or whatever.

But don't fret about it. Just focus on making it simple, fun, and just awesome. The tradition part will work itself out.

Whatever you share with your children isn't really important. It's how you go about it that makes it so great. Over the years, I've determined the key elements that make the Big Gulp a success.

So grab a drink, sit down, and get ready. Let me share with you The Way of The Big Gulp. And worry not, these wise words will quench the knowledge for which you thirst—how to create your own family's Big Gulp tradition!

Mystery

Catch your children off guard. Don't give them the slightest hint that something special is on the horizon. Be clever, get creative, and kick off the surprise in a cool way.

Routine

Collect a repertoire of simple, no-big-deal activities leading to a single, small surprise repeated periodically over time. From start to finish, never deviate from the plan. Otherwise the magic is lost. Your children will grow to love the ritual, the full experience. The end of the reward is just as important as the actions leading up to it. It has to be the exact same every single time. You want them to remember THAT Big Gulp. The way I remember my own.

Singularity

Make it a point to single out one child to take with you on the adventure. They need to feel special, like they're the only ones in this world enjoying such a magical, secret experience, whatever it may be. That it's just the two of you and no one else on the planet. They'll feel very important, very happy and very, very loved. Plus, they will have a blast.

(Years later, I found out I wasn't the only child in my family treated to a tasty Big Gulp and its equally rewarding adventure. But by this time, I was an adult, and understood why all of Gido's grandchildren got the same special treatment. As a child, however, I felt like I was the only one in on the adventure. And it was the adventure, the ritual, the approach and the secret just between the

two of us that made the Big Gulp so important).

Choice

Choice is paramount. It's always better when your children feel like they're making the decision. Give them two options. Dress one option up just well enough to make it more attractive than the other. You're essentially making the choice. But they won't know it. And in the end, the Big Gulp will be that much better.

Gido always told me that he was going to choose the Big Gulp for himself. He told me the candy bar made him too thirsty. My answer and the thought that went into it was really just a result of what he taught me. I didn't realize he could fit a lesson right there in the 7-Eleven. But "Gido knows!" it's can be done.

Speed

The process of them receiving this amazing Big Gulp should be quickly executed. Hours of waiting will wear the children out. Their patience will grow thin and their sense of anticipation will dissipate into a puddle of disinterest. Even a whole hour could be too much. Get in. Get out. Make them happy!

Gido always started this adventure with a quick nod of action. Before we had time enough to do anything but get excited, we were already there. He never told us in advance and I know that he planned it that way. The speed kept the excitement going!

Confidentiality

Don't let anyone else know what's going on. Make sure they

know that they're the only ones in on the secret. This keeps their little ears piqued for more information and their little brains intensely curious about the excitement on the horizon. Conspire with them. Tell them not to utter a peep of this adventure to anyone else. When they know it's a total secret, again, the Big Gulp is just that much sweeter.

I once asked Gido if my cousin could come. He said, in his playfully stern way, "Now, if I wanted everyone to come, do you think I would have invited everyone?" I answered with a now-obvious response, "yes." I quickly learned that the adventure was with me, and me alone!

Infrequency

You want to share a Big Gulp with your children enough to make them excited about it, often enough where they remember, but not so much that it loses its "cool factor." Like, just when they've almost forgotten about it, spring it on them out of nowhere.

My Gido and I experienced many Big Gulps together. Often enough for me to remember its thrill, but never often enough that I wasn't thrilled every time we went. It didn't happen all the time. And even when I sometimes thought we might go, we didn't. Basically, he kept it a mystery. The mystery of when we would get a Big Gulp made the Big Gulp legendary.

What's Your Big Gulp?

Now that we've cleared up a few good tips on how to work on your very own Big Gulp, it's time to put a name to it. What do you want your Big Gulp to be? The answer may come to you easily, something you already treat your children to every once in awhile, something you know they love but don't get to enjoy all that often—or often enough. And whether you have an idea or are completely without a clue, consider these few things:

Keep it Inexpensive

You don't want to break the bank. Find something simple. Simple most often means that it's light on the wallet (maybe a donut, a cupcake, a cookie, a baseball card, a hair ribbon.). And all dads know that a surprise that thrills your child and saves you money at the same time is definitely a win-win!

Make Sure it's Easily Accessible

Your Big Gulp needs to be close to home. Maybe a quick jaunt to your local gas station or even the mall or grocery store. Whatever it is, remember the mantra: "Get in. Get out. Make them happy!" Let's add "quickly!" to that list.

Make it Unique (Enough)

You want your Big Gulp to be out-of-the-ordinary to make the memory of it that much brighter in their minds. Special enough that it's an intrinsic element of their childhood memories. Don't make it so rare that you can't find it on a regular basis—like a special edition of-the-era toy collection. But you do want it to be cool enough that your child doesn't get exposed to it all that often.

Why This All Matters. Trust Me, it Actually Matters

A special drink. A candy bar. A pack of bubble gum. Whatever your Big Gulp ends up being, it's not about the actual "thing." It's about the just-you-and-me connection, the plan, the ritual, the thought, and the memory. It may not seem like a big deal at first. It may not even matter that much for a little while. But over time, as the months and years add up, your Big Gulp will be synonymous with your name, your face, and the way the fun made your child feel.

When my grandfather started sneaking me away and treating me to real Big Gulps, I was so small I could hardly reach above the counter to grab mine. The Big Gulp excursions with my Gido kept going, well into my teenage years.

I eventually found out that I wasn't the only one my grandfather discreetly whisked away for one-on-one Big Gulp getaways. By the time I did find out, I was an adult. And I realized that part didn't matter. My grandfather loved me very much. He loved my brothers, sisters, and my cousins very much, too. He taught us that love is an action. And it just took a small amount of time (and money) to show us how much he loved us and how special we were to him. No matter what, to each and every cousin, and on this and so many other similar occasions too many to even name, "Don't tell Grandma!"

This became one of his most popular quips. How especially threw the affectionate quote around when he wanted to let us think our innocent adventures and silly behaviors and hilarious moments with him were too much to let grandma in on. But of course, she always knew.

It always put a wide smile on all of our faces. And it still does. And that was the point.

All these years later, "Don't tell Grandma!" is still a punchline in the family—and is always used in the most loving way when he caps off an adventure or a conversation with us. It's his affection for her that makes it so funny. And again, he knows and we know that it's not meant to be a secret.

Just thinking about him saying it conjures a movie reel of memories. I think this is true for all of my family. He means the world to all of us. You'd think he'd hung the moon, as the saying goes, with the way we go on and on about our Gido.

Every Christmas, when everyone's sitting together, we inevitably get to one of his most famous punchlines. No matter the story, no matter who's telling it, my brothers, sisters, cousins, Gido, grandma, my parents—all of us—when the story's about to end, we all yell out, "Don't tell Grandma!" and laugh until we cry, loud and boisterous and full of joy and love.

My Gido will always be one of the most important people in my life, and our relationship one of the most meaningful. Not because we drank Big Gulps together, but because he loved me, and he showed it. And I felt it, even when I was too small to reach the counter. His love was an infinitely better reward than the Big Gulp.

Thank you, Grandfather.

"Gido knows!"

What My Son Said

Me: "Who wants to go today?"

My daughter: "I do!"

Me: "Oh, and he does too because he's raising both hands"

My son: "No dad, I'm just letting the A/C get to my armpits!"

Age: 7

CHAPTER 13

Moody Dad Syndrome (And The Man in the Mirror)

We were driving in the car. A buzzing, high-pitched—VOCALIZED—and irrational irritability—filled the entire space. There's a more concise word to describe it, and even the word itself, to most people, and especially to parents, generates an impossible, grating and, very rational sense of fully displayed and completely frayed nerves.

It's that horrible, torturous sound so many children make to get what they want or just to merely complain. It could almost be characterized as the word that must not be spoken. But I'll say it out loud. The word, get ready, is....

Whining.

First, it was too hot. Then, we weren't getting there fast enough. I didn't feel like there was an inkling of hope to change this almost unbearable and seemingly inescapable atmosphere in which I felt desperately trapped.

But then it got worse. Hunger set in.

Of course someone was hungry. As if the boiling heat and snail's pace of travel weren't infuriating enough, that awful beast known as hunger made its way into the already unbearable atmosphere, pretty much guaranteeing an even more tremulous trip that was *juuust* on the verge of causing full-blown emotional catastrophe.

The complaints and discontent just kept coming, like an unstoppable train. Nothing seemed to stop the incessant whining and practically vibrating irritability. No matter the destination, it didn't seem that anything could be done to quell the buzzing sense of a no-solution situation. The grumbles and sighs and all-around bad attitude started off in fairly few and somewhat intervals. But they grew rapidly into a grating noise and an almost endless litany of a severely unbearable monologue of anger and an all-around atmosphere I could barely stand.

While all of this was filling the entire atmosphere of our enclosed car, I adjusted my rear view mirror to take a look at my children. I figured that I owed it to myself to take a glimpse at my offspring—who have tested my patience on more occasions than I care to admit.

I tilted the mirror to get a full scope of the back seat and those unbearably cranky kids. It had to be them, right? Finally, a perfect view of the scene mere inches behind my driver's seat.

Were they fighting? *No.*

Were they frustrated? *Not even a little.*

Were they mad? *Not a chance.*

They looked up at me with innocence, with a stare that read

"why are you looking at us that way?"

Wait. What was going on here?

I replayed that internal monologue that I'd completely, and naturally, attributed to my children. Were they playing coy? I considered the heat, the travel time, and the lack of food. All three common challenges for children—and quite a trial on my children in particular.

I gave myself a timeout and turned my attention to the current situation. Our situation. This situation. Quickly rising tempers. A mounting anger I didn't know how to quell. But the children were calm. They were behaving. It was at that moment that I realized the issue.

It was me.

And hunger. And the heat. And the are-we-there yet, which was especially annoying, since I was driving and I KNEW how far away we were from "there."

More often than not, I'm in "the great dad" mood, the trusted leader, the one to help everyone forge ahead out of bad moods that let them enjoy the day and forget their worries and behave.

But on this day, I was most certainly not in "the great dad" mood, and I projected blame onto everyone around me. My children especially.

Sometimes our brains are not our friends. Usually when we're really irritable. We don't want to take the responsibility. Or rather, I can speak for myself, and say that that's definitely my personal experience.

My brain continued its unpleasant monologue. It told my conscience there was no way that *I* was the one to blame for all the crazy, full-to-bursting negativity filling up the car.

But I was.

I could not blame my children, no matter how much my mind wanted me to. My conscience won out. On that ride, at that moment, their daily leader, experienced a low leadership moment (hey, it happens!).

But that didn't mean I had to like it. My conscience knew the truth. But my brain refused to cooperate. I couldn't be responsible for all the chaos and drama running rampant within the confines of our car.

The facts won out, however. No out-of-control children were there to blame, it was just me in the midst of that low leadership moment.

Despite the madness I so quickly disbanded as "not my own," my children were watching every move I made, every word I said, every shake of my head, my hitting the steering wheel, and my constant whining.

I was on full display. And in these formative years, children soak their surroundings in like a sponge, and notice all the details and expressions and words and reactions and actions much,

much more than we give them credit for.

But this moment was just a single moment in their lives as they watched their father's behavior. During that moment and whenever you're around them, their brains notice what's happening and like a database, take mental pictures of every single one of my behaviors—storing it all in their easily accessible memory bank.

That's when daddy brain knocked Mr. Crankypants to the curb and assessed the full impact of this realization. My children watching my bad behavior was more than I could bear and more than their future and our relationship with as a family could really repair. This impact was huge.

My behavior's impact on my children was bigger and more important than just being in a bad mood and finally realizing you were the one to blame. That's very important.

But it wasn't as important as the impact my behavior had and has on my children. And this is the part I quickly realized that I had a bigger impact than anything.

I screwed up. I was acting like a baby! And, I needed to stop. Quickly!

The Real Impact

Parents say this to their kids a million times a day. "Stop acting like a baby!" they say. Often with fairly good reason. Many children truly act like toddlers long after their learning-to-walk-and-talk days are over. While this is a parental phrase I certainly don't condone, the problem here is less about those words and more about who it should be directed to.

Dads, especially. Our own "acting like a baby" behavior is on full display, and your children sit in the front row, experience all of your displayed, inappropriate, and even infantile emotions— played out right in front of their eyes. One very important impact of this behavior? They're taking mental notes, usually seated in their subconscious, etching it into an unseen action plan for their future behavior.

Did I just say "action plan for the future?" That's right! Your children see it all. Your behavior, good and bad, draws up a blueprint for how they'll walk and talk and to think and act in the future.

Think about it. Think about where your behavior—good and bad—came from. It came from what you saw in your formative years. How do you think children learn their behavior? From their everyday surroundings—friends, television and movies, teachers, other family members, and most importantly their parents. Dads, that means you, too. Especially you.

Do I have your attention now?

Parents—and dads most importantly—you are a powerful role model for your children. So, unless you want your children acting like babies for the rest of their lives, it's time to change. To stop acting like a baby, and to focus completely on being a good example for your children. It's time to stop acting like a baby!

Because sometimes, you just do! Admit it. I had to.

Adjust Your Mood. First

Before you can change your actions, you have to change your perspective, and your attitude. Before you can lead your life with a positive perspective and become a good example for your children, us dads need to discover and honestly address what is really going on here.

Our moods.

Moods are powerful, and shape our actions. When we're in a bad mood and we're letting it shape our behavior, it puts a damper on everything. Your children fall in line first into that "everything" category.

Now. Can you see the most important motivation for changing your negative attitude? Good. Let's continue.

Identify Why Your Mood is Sour. Because It Is

Moods develop from a plethora of circumstances. When you can identify the reason, look at the man the mirror. Just like that famous song says, "It's asking you to make a change." So instead of feeding into the negative mood and letting it run rampant, slow down. Identify why you're in this bad mood. Dads, for a minute, let's get really, really honest about ourselves.

What Kind of Mood Man Are You?

The "Feed-Me-Now" Man

You need a sated appetite before you're strong and resilient enough to behave yourself. As your fuel decreases and you start running on empty, your senses become dull and impatient. And so does your attitude. You tend to get grouchy the most right around a meal time. "I must eat now. RIGHT NOW", is all your mind and body can say. And of course, the kids need snacks first, before you have the chance to eat. And. YOU HAVE TO MAKE THE DINNER YOU SO DESPERATELY DESIRE. The mere thought of dishing out satisfying snacks to your children before you get your own food reward results in a serious shift of impatience, frayed nerves, and a swiftly increasing (bad) temper. You go back to cave-man mode. You sometimes even resort to grunts until you yourself get food. Almost as if the food is controls you. And your mood.

The "It's-Way-Too-Hot-Inside-Outside-and-Everywhere" Man

When temperatures rise above 85 degrees, your attitude changes immediately. And it's not the positive kind. It's not like you don't like and enjoy the heat and the shining sun. It's great a lot of the time—like at the beach—but only if you plan on it, specifically seek it, and limit it to manageable time periods. Trying to get your children in order during the hotter times can make your mood steam without advanced warning. You even think your children need to be put "in line" when really you should pull out a mirror to identify the real issue.

The "I-Need-5-More-Minutes-of-Sleep" Man

Waking you early makes you more than groggy. Irritable is a better word that for it. Groggy and irritable is not a good combination. You'll daydream of the days before you had children. Even though you love your children. But at this moment, you can't quite think about that. You also try to grab a nap while your children are napping and then tell them "it's not time to get up" if when you yourself want to nap longer. Your pillow becomes your best friend—especially when you're tired.

The "I'm-Not-Good-Until-I-Have-My-Coffee" Man

The sweet, sweet jolt of coffee, here, is your saving grace, the jumpstart you need to function like a nice, normal human being. In fact, it's more than a jump start, it's a necessity. It means much more than a tasty beverage for a little morning boost. It's an indisputable REQUIREMENT in the morning. Your children can easily wake you up, but that's nowhere near enough to get you going. Coffee rules your morning routine. And when you miss it, EVERYONE knows it!

The "I'm-in-the-Middle-of-Something" Man

It's not necessarily the interruption that makes things go bad. It's more about the lack of patience that throws things out of whack. You react negatively without pausing until the moment you're ready to respond in a rational and caring manner. This is what bothers you. You don't feel like you have time to do all the work it takes to be reasonable. You feel like you need a breather from your surroundings. And when you can't get a breather, you can't focus. A shift in that focus can cause you to, well, lose it.

Your words are less filtered during interruptions, even if you're usually soft-spoken most of the time.

The "I-Just-Got-Home-from-Work-Give-Me-Quiet" Man

The first 30 minutes when you get home from work is paramount to the success of the rest of the night for you. But only when there is quiet time. And for you, that means absolute quiet. No exciting news. No news at all. No words. Even beyond quiet time is the relaxation time. The stress-free time. And the unwind time. You need your space immediately upon arrival, otherwise—to put it nicely, you're not exactly welcoming toward anyone who dares enter your comfort zone. And let's face it, "not welcoming" is a far-too-generous term for your demeanor.

The "Can't-You-See-the-Game-is-On" Man

Sports are a serious event. Not some fun show that just magically happens to show up on the tube. It's planned. And I mean PLANNED. You know the date, the time, the channel—sometimes weeks in advance. You look forward to it daily. It's serious. It's important. You know those game days as soon as the season schedule was released. They're happening for you. You've got the dates etched in your brain. Many don't understand that this is not almost deadly serious—except your family.

You don't EVER keep your eyes off the television in fear of a missed play. Usually the sport, the game—is football, but can easily extend to baseball, basketball, or hockey. If your team is not on, you frantically search for another—even if you don't care for the team. A game has got to be ON. And you've got to see it. This is non-negotiable. When the game is playing, life is on pause. Speaking of pause, the remote is off-limits because that is YOURS. And when someone tries to unpause life, you can get more fired up than the losing coach.

The "Work-was-Awful-So-Everything-is-Awful" man

The success or stress of your work day is directly proportional to the peace and harmony your family enjoys. When you have a good day, all is well. When your day went badly, discord and discomfort reign over the night. You even pray for a good day so you can have a good night. You have a hard time separating your work mindset from your off-site mindset. You don't leave work at home. And even if you do have to bring work home, it's the attitude about it that trips you up. The emotional line between home and work is fuzzy at best. You don't care for your job most days, and your emotional effusion lets your family know that, which leads to a whole 24-hours of stress. They know you don't like your job—not just because you say it, but because your actions towards them make it obvious, and compound your frustrations with yourself, your family and your life. Life in the job department—and hence, the life department—just isn't great. And everyone knows it.

What's Happening?

A poison of sorts over which we don't yet have the antidote. Not yet anyway, but it is available. First, the poison—the strange phenomenon that can best be described with the well-known story of Doctor Jekyll and Mr. Hyde. No matter your poison—whether one listed above or one you're slowly starting to recognize in your own life—you're plagued with an Achilles heel in the great dad realm, a strange phenomenon in which you resemble your normal self but little.

One in which you're brusque, inconsiderate, selfish, rude, and thoughtless—only when the poison triggers you. Otherwise you are usual, loving, calm, patient, and fun self—even during sporadic and chaotic times that don't fit into your known triggers. Your true self is caring and focused upon your children's needs when they don't fit into one of the above listed categories. Dads don't necessarily fit in all of these zones—wow, that would be awful—but at some point in your day or your week, inevitably, the categories above—at least one—will trigger your moody-dad downfall.

But what is it?

What causes grown dads—intelligent dads—to transform without warning from great, happy dads to peevish and impatient dads whose behavior is the exact opposite of their normal disposition?

I call it "Daddy-Baby Syndrome."

(Get it? I've transposed "Baby-Daddy," to "Daddy-Baby Syndrome." Pretty darn clever if I do say so myself. And obviously, I do. Nevertheless, let's get down to just what it means to experience "Daddy-Baby Syndrome.")

Disclaimer
I am 100-percent, absolutely, positively, NOT a doctor. I cannot prescribe medicine. Well, I really can't prescribe anything for that matter.

So, as you continue to read, please consult a REAL doctor if you are experiencing nausea, vomiting, red eyes, a swollen neck, constant headaches, chronic fatigue or anything else you claim is "natural." I'm fairly confident these symptoms mean that you are just a dad now. You're extra-busy with much, much more going on in your life than you could have ever imagined until you became a father. If you thought your life was busy and hectic before children, you know now that life before parenthood was much simpler than you thought.

You are not sick; you're a parent. A dad. Terminally.

Thanks to my marketing-industry career, "Daddy-Baby Syndrome" is simply a catchy, clever phrase that sums all of these behaviors we've been exploring. I've based this easy-to-remember-and-of-course-clever nomer merely on personal observation—mainly of myself.

Allow me to warn you that continued reading from this sentence forward may result in a renewed sense of recognizing and taking responsibility for your own "daddy-baby" behaviors along with, but not limited to, a more sympathetic mindset, a love-inspired game plan to change your behaviors, possibly an apology and living amends to those family members most affected by your infantile behavior, a strong and healthy awareness of your future actions and reactions as they arise in your life and extreme patience. This is a simplified list. Many other side-effects may occur.

"Daddy-Baby Syndrome" Affects Almost All Dads

Symptoms may arise immediately in some dads, while other dads experience a more gradual onset. Sometimes these symptoms last for minutes while others extend for numerous hours, some exceeding more than 24 hours or extending into a period of multiple days.

Remember that "Daddy-Baby Syndrome" is merely an experience of sporadic changes in mood, usually the result of a variety of triggers as yet beyond your control. Remember, the onset and continued experience of "Daddy-Baby Syndrome" does NOT mean you are a bad dad. However, if left untreated, these fluctuating changes in mood can poorly affect all aspects of your life, most importantly, the current and future well-being and happiness of your children.

Take "Daddy-Baby" Steps to Improve Mood

Just like anyone going through a difficult time, there are easy steps available to all dads who have the desire to regain their "superhero" status and manage or even eliminate the moody overtones and undertones that occur when left unchecked.

These steps are pretty complicated. They're long. They're tedious.. You may even feel so daunted by their complexity that you'll feel hopeless to recover from "Daddy-Baby Syndrome." The task at hand is definitely an uphill battle to recover the fresh focus you're looking for as a dad. You must be willing to go to any length to stay a fresh and focused father. If you are, you are ready to take these essential steps.

They are as follows:

1. **Recognize that you are moody.**
2. **Make a conscious decision to change your mood.**

Okay, I was kidding a bit. So yes. Two steps. Just two. Not more. Let's keep it simple, dads. We do NOT need a long list for how to come out of our moody funk. Again, it's simple.

Of course we are going to be stressed at times. Of course circumstances will alter our moods. We're not perfect. Our goal, of course, is to be a great dad and help create a harmonious family environment. But let's keep it simple. That's just the given goal, the result of meeting your above-listed goals while maintaining a pleasant and acceptable mood and behavior. Even following these steps, I know I'm definitely never going to be perfect all the time.

We can get better, however. We need to ask ourselves one simple question to help us determine whether or not we're going to stay moody:

Is being moody really worth it?

First, what is your goal? If your goal is to have a few minutes of quiet time when you get home, politely ask your family for a little time to unwind when you come home from work every day. If you want to watch the game, show consideration for your family and communicate this plan well ahead of time so everyone knows what to expect and plan their own day around it, too.

Do you want coffee and need it bright and early to stay positive and just simply kind? Then set your coffee on automatic-brew before bed. Do you need your space when you are trying to focus on work or other important obligations? Equip your house and rearrange its space so you have a quiet, private place your family knows not to disturb while you're in there. Don't make the house "shut down" because you need quiet. Seek quiet elsewhere.

These are examples only. Ones that work for me. They may not be your answers to correct what you need to stay away from "Daddy-Baby Syndrome." But to be successful and make your own life and your family life happy and smooth, you do need to find out what makes you moody, and what you can do to correct the triggers that make you that way.

And if you're unaware of your dark cloud of moody, why not try asking someone?

One Day, I Asked My Children

Later on in the day of my fabled terrible-no-good-very-bad

drive for which I alone was responsible, I was again driving down the road with my children in the backseat. But this time, it was a calm ride. It was after dinner, so we were pleasantly full, on our way home, their energy already spent after a long day.

Just like before, I glanced in the rear-view window and scanned their faces. Casually gazing out of their respective windows, they were not talking with each other. Not even cracking each other up, as they tend to do. They were just content.

I thought this was a good opportunity to ask my children an important question.

"Do you think I'm moody a lot?"

I made sure to set this question carefully. I wanted them to be honest. And I needed them to feel safe doing so. Normally, adult questions like that feel like set-ups to kids. It's a balancing act for them. I mean, what child will quickly blurt out exactly how they feel about their dad's moods? After all, moods have put them in precarious positions in the past.

"No matter what you say, you will not be punished," I said.

After all, I wanted to make sure they were going to be honest. Completely honest. I wanted sincerity more than I wanted obedience. Just for that moment, at least.

My daughter was reluctant to answer. But she did speak up first. With a hesitant mumble. "Yes," she uttered in an almost whisper, looking to the side and seeming to speak more to herself than to me.

"It's OK, you can tell me," I smiled, replying quickly in a fast effort to ease her clear discomfort.

I could see she was nervous. My daughter has always been known as the "comforter" of the family and watches carefully how she speaks to others.

Quickly after that, my son—who is never afraid to say anything, to anyone, at any time—said in a sly voice, "Yeah, Dad...a lot!"

Wow!

I don't consider myself "dad of the year," of course. I also don't like of myself as a perfect dad by any means. But, I did consider myself a good dad.

This blatantly honest feedback—that I was not only most definitely moody, but moody A LOT took me way off-guard. I did ask for it, though. And I was thankful for their unfiltered truth.

I was moody! And often. I knew what I had to do.

Put Pride Aside and Apologize

Oh, and remember when I said you only needed two steps to ensure a complete "Daddy-Baby Syndrome" recovery. Well, there's actually one more.

3. Apologize.

Once you've completely realized, confirmed with outside parties, and accepted in no uncertain terms what triggers your unpleasant behavior, you're finally ready to take the final step, come full circle, and get back on track. It's pretty easy really. As long as you're not too prideful. Step three: apologize.

And that's exactly what I did.

Handling the Truth (Our Road Trip Story, Continued)

Once my children honestly disclosed that I was moody—A LOT—I found myself face-to-face with an important decision. I could continue on as if I were never moody, never acted inappropriately, and that no mention of the black cloud that sometimes hangs over my head had ever been made.

That would be EASY, right? I'm DAD, after all. I run this place. What I say GOES (usually). It could be all too easy to throw my weight around and pretend like I'd never heard a word.

But that just wasn't the right move.

Back to the car and the driving and our never ending road trip that is our circuitous path to and from home and school and work and church and everywhere, really.

"I have something to tell you," I said. They quickly averted their attention to the front of the car.

"I'm sorry!!"

Pause. (A quick one.)

"Do you forgive me?" I asked.

OK. Get Back on Track!

The "Daddy-Baby Syndrome" recovery process can be quick or slow. But while you have a good bit to process, it doesn't take a lot of time. Unless you let it. And why waste time when you want to get back on track to a happier dad, happier children, and a happier family life?

The steps are easy as 1-2-3.

1. Identify your moods and what causes them.
2. Change the root cause of your negative behaviors.
3. Apologize to the people affected by your bad moods.

So whether you rip it off like a band-aid or keep drawing it out, the only thing that matters in the end is that YOU DID IT.

Here's How Our Story Ended

After I apologized to my children, there was a brief pause.

I didn't know what to expect. They'd been no-holds-barred honest with me before that honestly, I had absolutely no idea what to expect from them when I humbly asked for forgiveness from these small humans. My children.

I then heard one simple word from them all.

"YES!"

I was overjoyed to hear them say this. I was grateful.

Your Way or the Highway. Not So Fun

At this point, you've started to think about your own "dark cloud" triggers and their resulting very-bad moods. And now—thank goodness—know that in just three easy steps, you can get back on track and be the superhero dad who leads with ease, rather than the one that is moody, and frequently.

And right now, you have a choice. You can carry your mood into the way that you lead your children. You can lead your children based on rules, and rules alone. Or, you can lead them with positivity (with a better mood) and incorporate rules along the way. This is the way that I recommend. I've done both, but only one works. Effectively.

It's easier to drop your mood and lead with a positive attitude. Make it easier on everyone. Your children will be WILLING to follow your lead instead of just choosing to do what you asked because they know they have to.

The choice is yours.

CHAPTER 14

The First Rule About Fight Club

I was in the fourth grade. After spending my entire young life in the sunny state of Florida, I now found myself in the swamp-filled state of Louisiana. And it was my first year in a new school.

I was in the prime of my elementary school days and walked that schoolyard with confident swagger. My grades were borderline amazing, I had finally learned how to comb my hair to perfection, and I was proud to be known as "that kid who can catch any pop fly" in kickball.

Life was pretty awesome.

The bell rang. This was a good sound. I reflexively tightened my grip on my lunchbox, ready to fight my way through the classroom door. I rushed to the lunchroom. Most children dove into their yummy lunches with happy smiles on their faces. And while I never complained about eating the nicely cut peanut butter and jelly sandwich my mom put into my lunch each day, my attentions were focused on what came right after lunch.

Recess

You know, the playground. Freedom. A time to run. To scream. To yell. To go crazy. Best of all? We could get away with it. We could get away with every last bit of it. Our teachers encouraged it. Sitting in their worn, plastic and broken-in-some-small-way-

or-another chairs, their concern focused solely on battling it out for the few and far between glimpses of shade, hiding as best they could from the relentless, blistering sun.

I'm not sure if the heat was so bad because it was Louisiana or what. But I was used to hot. I was from the Sunshine State, after all.

Our particular playground, however, wasn't what you'd call the usual sand and swings and trees kind of deal. It wasn't quite normal. Picture a massive field. I mean MASSIVE. That was our playground.

Smack dab in the center were the basketball courts—dark black with faded lines outlining a semblance of boundaries. The metal rims offered no give, no bend. Not even a little. This pretty much meant you had to be a sharp-shooter before you dared to enter the game. And I was no sharp-shooter. I rarely touched foot there.

Beyond the basketball court?

The entire country. A map of it anyway—a gargantuan map of the entire United States encompassing about 100 feet in diameter. Or so it seemed, who knows how big it *really* was. I was small. And that makes everything large, even more so in memory. We called the place the "states," and this was where the marbles games happened. And we played for keeps. It was a pretty serious endeavor.

The Object of the Game

Three of your own marbles were placed inside a specified area. Your opponent placed three of their own marbles in. Each player took a turn flicking their own marble into the full set of marbles, with the intent to hit your marbles outside of the originally designated area.

The Rules Were Simple

The first player to get the most out, won—and the winner walked away with all of the marbles.

We didn't realize it was a form of gambling back then, but it was fun. Our principal, however, knew it was gambling, and when she caught anyone playing them, the players lost all of their marbles, hahaha.

(Us kids weren't crazy, but some of us wondered whether or not she was. Anyway, I was raised to know that name-calling was no good, so we'll leave that there.)

We heard a lot of rumors about what she did with those marbles. No one really knew. But, you always left either happy with a bunch of marbles clinking around in your pockets—or you left disappointed, pockets empty.

Now. To the *far* right of the basketball court—a two-to-three-minute-jog far—was our kickball field. This was my turf. This was where I shined. I was the man. The star. The athlete.

My friends—the sharp-shooters on the courts and the marble

aficionados—mainly stayed close to the courts and the "states." So it was just me out there, away from my buddies, but that never mattered. I was there to uphold my name. Everyone knew my name. My name was Chris. Chris Bultman. Did they know that? Nope. I had one name out there— the "kid who can catch any pop fly!"

I got the name pretty quickly. Each day kids lined up to get picked for a team. The same two boys were always the captains. They owned that place. They picked their friends and then picked their friends' friends. If you weren't already their friend, you pretty much were never picked. But one day, I lined up in my purple jeans shorts ready to play. The de rigueur friends-picking practice remained the same. But this was my day. They didn't have enough of their friends that day to fill their team. The last spot was between me and another boy. I didn't know who they were going to pick. Before they made their selection, the captain asked me who could catch a kickball in the air. I wanted to answer. I did.

I'm not sure if it was because the captain looked about three grades ahead of me (he wasn't) or if it was because he was about seven-feet-tall (he wasn't) or if he was stronger than anyone in the world (clearly, he wasn't, but I thought he was), but I was pretty intimidated.

In these situations, kids usually act in one of two ways. First, they freeze in their tracks and go silent. Second, they do what I did. I threw up my hand and yelled "meeeee!" in an almost out-of-body reflex and I couldn't believe I said it.

But I did, and I got picked for his team. I ended up in the outfield and caught three consecutive flyballs at the end of the game to seal the win for our team. No matter what requirements you consider necessary to be called a hero don't apply right now. Because on this day catching three consecutive flyballs for my team made me a hero. From then on I was well-known for this very heroic skill.

I was "the kid who could catch any flyball." That's right, I've told you three times already.

So that was our recess world. Our playground. Big field. Basketball. Marbles. Kickball. Teachers hiding from the heat. Each activity a world unto its own, thanks to that massive field encompassing a truly great and expansive (if a bit unusual) place for kids to play.

Then Suddenly, Everything Changed

It started out like every other day, with kids heading straight to their usual spots. I was strolling across the open field to uphold my status on the kickball field when suddenly I heard a whistle.

This sound signaled a change—not just on the playground. This whistle set off a series of events that changed the way I learned how parents should protect their children.

It went a little something like this.

The Principal's Office

I don't remember how I got there, I just remember being there. It was a dreaded place, and when you were there it usually meant bad news. Or much worse.

The principal's office.

I stood by the far right side wall. It wasn't a big office, even for being so small I remember that. She had a big, sturdy, wooden desk. As I stared at the desk something glimmering caught my eye. From the lamplight on her desk, I caught a glimpse. A clear vase containing something I treasured. We all treasured them.

OUR MARBLES!

"Ah, so this is where the marbles found their resting spot," I thought to myself. But it wasn't the only casing that held these treasures. She had another small containers on her desk and a medium sized one on a stand behind her desk. It was the marble graveyard. The rumors were true, and my nerves *trembled*.

I was busted. At long last, all those days of my guileless, innocent game of unbeknownst-to-me-actual *gambling* my marbles away finally came crashing down all around me. I stood in her office along with about five other boys who seemed to share a similar fate. Getting in trouble, a pretty stressful experience in elementary school—almost the scariest fate of every single school-aged kid in the known universe.

I looked at the boys lined up beside me, and suddenly it struck me: these guys weren't marble players. A few owned the basketball courts...and woah, my kickball captain—a guy who helped me make a real name for myself on that playground.

Why were these guys here?

More importantly, *what was I doing here?*

The principal, after a nerve-wracking wait that seemed also to be part of the punishment, entered the room with a swift, startling gait and a cold-as-ice aspect, matching the chilling atmosphere us young children found ourselves in. No greeting. She didn't even say hello. Though that office gleamed with a million marbles, there was not a hint of a sparkle in her eyes even though the marbles glowed like a halo for boys like me. They were treasures to us. But today, those gleaming marbles couldn't even spark a flickering glimmer of light.

She finally spoke, her cold and stern face in perfect tune with her words—and she KEPT talking and talking. No kindness, no compassion, no attempt to do anything to discipline with calmness and logic—as I'd always experienced when I behaved against my father's expectations. She intended to scare us. And she looked down upon us as if we were bad children instead of young kids who had possibly made a poor decision.

She pointed out forcefully that we were in really big trouble for how bad we'd been—so bad that our parents we're called upon to come to our school and discuss our bad behavior further.

Next up? A tiny version of my dad sat upon my shoulder. You know, the type of thing where you normally see your good and bad conscience sitting on either side? But this was only my dad. He told me what to do in that moment—and it was based on what he'd already taught me:

> *If you're getting blamed for something you didn't do, you have*
> *nothing to be nervous about. If you're innocent, you have no*
> *need to be afraid. If you don't know why you're in trouble,*
> *ask. It's okay to seek an answer. The answer gives a discordant*
> *situation clarity, and hopefully, harmony.*

As I stood in front of our principal, I was reminded of this advice. I was young, but my dad taught me well. He taught me to think about the situation I was in—any situation I was in—and assess it. Figure out what was going on and if I didn't know, try to get some answers.

Up until this point, I didn't have any answers. I was standing in the principal's office, assuming that I was the next marble victim. But I clearly wasn't. She spoke in generalities about how bad we were. She never specified why, but everyone knew exactly what she was talking about.

Except me.

When she finally took a breath from her general and ad nauseum lecture, I mustered up the courage to raise my hand.

"Do you have something to say, Mr...."

"Chris, Chris Bultman," I said, almost referring to myself as the "boy who could catch any popup." After all, the captain was giving me the eye and I didn't want to let him down.

"What do you have to say for yourself?" she barked.

"What am I doing here?"

I asked as nicely and properly as I could. Not a hint of the sarcasm that often crept into my tone at that age. I was a good kid but did have a tendency to think I was always right. But this time I couldn't be "right" because I didn't even know what was going on.

I felt my father's age-old and deep-seated wisdom resonate within me. I heard his voice in my mind, once again giving me the lessons I'd learned about situations just like these. And I followed through with his advice. I asked a question. And I waited for my answer. My dad was my dad and he wasn't ever wrong, I thought to myself.

I finally got my answer!

"Don't play dumb with me, you know exactly why you are here!"

As she spoke, I discovered a truth that has stuck with me all the way into my own fatherhood years.

Don't assume a child knows an answer to a question they are asking.

I was in the principal's office. I didn't know why I was there. I remembered my dad's advice. I took his advice. But, following his sage wisdom did not play out how I hoped it would—or how he told me it would.

A Conversation with My Dad

Once again, I found myself standing at attention in front of a concerned adult, a feeling not dissimilar to my recent experience in the principal's office. I'd given my mom the school's sealed envelope, addressed to my parents, a few hours earlier.

The envelope. I had no idea what it contained. It read: "To the parents of Christopher Bultman."

Even though I didn't know what was inside that sealed envelope, I knew it was serious. It looked official. From the tightness of the seal to the formality with which it addressed my parents. So official that my thoughts didn't even wander the consideration of opening it before I handed it to my mom. And I handed it to her as soon as I got home from school.

And now my dad had the letter in his hand. He was sitting down at the end of his bed as I stood, nearly eye-to-eye with him. I knew an equal eye level meant that we were about to have a serious conversation.

"Did you do it?"

His tone was direct and inquisitive.

"Do what?" I responded. I truly didn't know what was going on. I hadn't known what was going on in the principal's office even though I followed my father's advice to always ask questions when I needed clarification. And I was still left in the dark. But now that I was standing in front of him, I used his technique again. At least in my head.

And there it was again.

My little conscience. Speaking to me. Again, it was in the form of my dad. My influence. The guy who taught me most of what I know.

He was saying:

> *Of course you can ask me a question. You can ask me any question. Your questions should get you answers. Your answers will give you understanding. Your understanding will help guide your next steps. Your next steps should always be taken with the right purpose. Your purpose should always be to seek truth.*

"Dad, I don't know what's in the envelope. I was in the principal's office and tried to find out but she ignored my question. Can you tell me?"

I said this in an honest tone. I didn't know what was going on which was frustrating me. I needed answers and hoped my dad would tell me what was going on.

He told me that all of the parents of the students who'd been in the principal's office with me would be attending a school meeting for a very terrible act. The bad act: the boys had opened a drainage covering in the middle of the recess field with the explicit intention to shove some of the other kids into that hole.

What? Really? I was clueless. I didn't do this. I had no part of this. I didn't know this was even going on. I didn't know that these kids were causing trouble.

I went from the emotion of cluelessness to a rush of do-I-think-my-dad-will-believe-me-when-I-tell-him-I-didn't-do-it thoughts.

"I didn't do it!" I blurted out. I said it with confidence, with conviction, and with strong emotion. It was the truth. I meant it. And I wanted my dad to know it.

First, he paused. After a second or two he spoke very calmly and slowly.

"Are you telling me the truth?"

"Yes."

"Are you absolutely sure you're telling me the truth?"

"Yes."

Then he responded with something I will never forget.

"OK, that's all I needed to hear." He said.

And then, our conversation was over.

The Meeting

The time span between the conversation with my dad to the arrival at the school felt like a snap of a finger. It was quick. I don't remember getting to the meeting. I just remember being there.

This time, we were in a bigger room with a conference table. Its dark wood matched the principal's office furniture, which was fresh in my mind. Perhaps it was those shiny marbles that made it stand out so much.

As I glanced around the room, I saw the boys who'd stood with me in military fashion the day before, already ready for their punishment because, unlike me, they knew what they'd done and why they were in that office. Today, they sat next to their parents with the same guilty look in their eyes I'd seen earlier.

I was also sitting by my dad. He sat patiently, arms folded, his back against the chair.

It wasn't a position of comfort, it was a position of command. He was waiting.

Then the voice reappeared.

> *Always sit properly when addressing someone. People take you more seriously if they know you handle yourself properly. Dress the part. Look the part. And most importantly, speak the part.*

At every stage of the game, I kept recalling the little tidbits of information my dad had taught me. Except this time I was seeing it come to fruition. He played nearly every card he'd taught me. And I was seeing it first hand. He didn't need to use words to tell me what was going to happen because his actions spoke it loud and clear.

The stance he held caused me to sit up straighter in my chair. He didn't tell me to. I just did it. I didn't *think* I had to, I knew I had to. Something was about to happen. I wasn't quite sure what, but I was reading the signs and I knew it was about to go down.

A moment later, the principal walked into the room. She circled the entire room to reach the head of the table. She was the last person to enter the room. My gut told me she did this for effect, making sure to mark the same authority she displayed less than 24 hours earlier.

I knew that look. My dad had the same look in his eyes.

The principal spoke. The parents of the students spoke. And even some of the students spoke.

But my dad sat there. His look didn't change. The way he sat in the chair didn't change. He displayed patience. And a lot of it.

> *Don't rush your words if you want to be taken seriously. Be patient. Wait for the right opportunity. When you do speak, speak directly. With confidence, and clarity. Speak with purpose. And make sure you always, and I mean always, maintain direct eye contact with whom you're speaking to.*

The principal turned to my dad and signaled for a response

from him. Like a calm lion, he positioned himself from relaxed confidence to a stance of unspoken power. He uncrossed his arms, leaned forward, placing them firmly on the table. Everyone shifted. We could all feel his power. We knew he was about to speak. With commanding authority.

My dad talked for a few minutes. To be completely honest, I don't remember much of what my dad said. But I do remember one thing.

"My son didn't do it!"

He said this without an ounce of doubt. Without a waiver of uncertainty. He believed what he said and meant it. No one in that room, not even the principal, came close to the strength of his authority that day.

I don't remember anything else he said. Except that.

"My. Son. Didn't. Do. It."

Those words have never left me. Not that day. Not ever.

What I told him the night before were words that he trusted. He listened to me. He believed me. He stood by me.

It meant a lot to me.

The words in my head sounded like this:

> Trust your children when they say they are telling the truth. Listen to them if they are trying to tell you something. And stand up for them if someone is coming against them. Be their shield. They will learn from this and teach their own children when they are ready.

My dad looked down at me and said three words.

"We are going."

He said it calmly. But I knew he was serious.

We stood up and left the meeting.

The Respect

I don't remember talking much as we drove home. I sat there thinking about what happened. I knew what my dad did for me that day. He defended me when I told him I didn't do it.

The next morning, I got up to get ready for school. I grabbed my backpack and headed toward the door, ready to catch the school bus. Just as I was almost outside, my dad asked to speak with me.

He kneeled down to talk to me, once again getting on my eye

level. He explained to me that there were a lot of boys from school who did a bad thing. He told me that they wouldn't be at school today because of what they did.

I asked him why I was allowed to go to school.

"Because, you didn't do it!"

I smiled. It was a great feeling. I had someone in my corner.

Remember the first rule? The first rule about fight club? We don't talk about it. We don't mention anything. To anyone. At any time. Not once. Not ever. This same rule applied here. With my dad. So, I never said a word.

Before he let me go, he said "please don't discuss this at school."

His words were simple but much portent lay within them:

> *Just because we were right, doesn't mean we go around talking about it to everyone. We can show respect to people like the principal even though she was wrong. We keep our business our business and keep it within the walls of our home. Gossiping doesn't help anyone. It never does. It never will.*

I knew what he was saying even though he didn't say it.

I left for school that day as if nothing ever happened.

Protect Your Children

What started as an innocent day of me trying to keep my fame on the kickball field alive turned into a series of crazy events that landed me in the principal's office, ending in my dad protecting me from the false accusation of my own wrongdoing.

He didn't have to take the time to do what he did. He didn't have to say what he said. And he didn't need to do it the way that he did.

But he chose to. And he chose to do it for me.

You don't always need to sit down with your children and go over a list of rules, or items that they need to learn, or speak to them directly about what they need to do. Sometimes your actions can be an appropriate substitute for all of those things.

Your actions speak much louder than your words.

Thanks, Dad.

CHAPTER 15

The Dad Life

Throughout this book, you've been introduced, or even re-introduced to all kinds of parenting concepts you probably already know about—and hopefully, you'll find some new and useful tools that will up your dadhood game big time.

This is a serious book written in a casual and humorous style. Remember, being a dad is the most important thing you'll do in your life. It will also be filled with adventures you can't help but laugh at—and despair about, and cry about, and rejoice about, and wear yourself out to the bone about.

But it's all worth it. More than worth it. Your children are your life. And your life is your children. I'm a dad. Just because I've written a book about fatherhood does not mean I'm an expert. I'm full of flaws and missteps and have fallen and failed, but I've always gotten back up again, determined always to do a better job—to be the best dad I can be—for my children.

I'm no expert. I'm a dad. Just like you. And I simply want to share the tools I've picked up along the way as I grow with my children as a dad—and live the Dad Life.

I've made sure to let you in on the ideas and experiential lessons I personally find essential to good fatherhood. Stories I've lived through—the kinds of stories you're probably already familiar with—and the methods I've been taught by my own father and his father and from my own progression as a dad.

The topics in this book cover a variety of my own experiences—ones you're probably familiar with, too. They're about the very soul-deep convictions and ideals and methods that guide me on the path toward becoming the best father I can be. To become a father of integrity, strength, honor, and dignity (internally, now—no dad can be seen, in action, as dignified all the time—but you know what I mean).

I want to take you along for the ride. Part storybook, part reference book, I've written #DadLife to share with you what I've learned and what I try to do every day to become the best father I can be.

The parenting methods I've written about in this book are designed to help you make your life as a dad have a powerful and lasting impact on your children for the rest of their lives—even into their own parenthood.

Adding a little humor into the mix doesn't hurt either. After all, children are pretty hilarious, and so is fatherhood. Hopefully, this book has brought back experiences and lessons you've already learned in your life as a dad, and my wish is that you'll find that you're not alone on this adventure and that there are answers and methods you can turn to to help you during your adventure.

But we've still got a question, don't we? I do. And I'll do my best to answer it for you. And for me, too.

What does living The Dad Life really mean? There's got to be a method to the madness. I think I've found it.

What is the Dad Life?

As I began writing this book, I didn't have a clear definition of how to clearly communicate what the "Dad Life" really means. And after I found myself re-writing the introduction to this book about ten times, it became even more evident.

I wanted to create a concrete definition of Dad Life. One that could easily be understood, quickly communicated, and just simply made sense.

After giving it some thought, I've finally hit the nail on the head and come up with a simple definition.

Dad Life: The life a man leads for his children.

This definition sums it up. Again, it's pretty simple. Any guy who has children is a dad. That's a given. But when he *consciously leads his life for his children*, that's what I consider a Dad Life.

Leading it for his children? What does this mean? To live his life with explicit purposes: to guide them with strong morals; to teach them more than what is required; to protect them in all situations; and to love them beyond measure. The list goes on and on. But the key thing here is that this Dad Life dad's primary life focus is on his children. Whatever life choices he makes, no matter how big or small, they're intentional. They're considered carefully. And are always focused on how these choices impact his children. He lives with intention.

But as I starting to explore this phrase ("Dad Life") more deeply, I discovered it was far more complex and nuanced than simple intentions. There had to be action, too. There had to be a method. A way. Behind every successful dad, there had to be a combined way of life—of action, intention, method, and purpose—that made them so effective and exemplary.

I tried to figure out what drives us dads to live an intentionally passionate life for our children. To want to be there for them unconditionally—even when we are stressed, exhausted, and even at our wit's end with them—no matter what.

This "Dad Life" is more than just a life for our children; it is a calling, and it's a way of life for ourselves, too. I get butterflies in my stomach. A spark in my heart. A warmth and thrill within— an amazing feeling of purpose. As soon as my children were born I was excited to lead my children. Daily. To teach them. Mentor them. Guide them. Cry with them. Fail with them. And succeed with them.

But I still struggled to explain exactly how to live a great Dad Life. Partly because people asked me what it meant. But most importantly: I just didn't have a clear answer. How could I make it make sense? How could I make it quantifiable? How could I transform my intangible feelings and thoughts about my "Dad Life"—my passion for living the best life possible for my children—into a something tangible?

And more specifically, how do I explain this besides some of the obvious things like: I like to make them peanut butter and jelly sandwiches; I'll clean up after them even when I'm busy; and I like to tuck them in at night.

It's not like there is a secret formula or hidden recipe that could make someone else life the best life they can as a dad.

Or *is* there?

I started to examine some of my role models—my dad, grandfather, uncle, brother, and pastor. The people I've been around a lot. Whose behavior I've had the privilege to see first-hand. Dads who lead their children in a way that I truly admire. I knew I could use my insight into their ways of life to explain how to live a great Dad Life to other people.

Did they share similar traits? Did they do things the same way or did their methods differ? What was it about their actions that made me think they lived a great and desirable type of Dad Life?

This formula is easy. Its purpose is to help you become the best dad you can. No dad is perfect. No dad will ever be perfect. (C'mon, we all know there is no such thing. Just take me as an example.) This formula isn't flawless (we know that every formula in history has exceptions. You know, variations that make the formula mean nothing. Or explode. Or fizzle over. You know, that scientific stuff.). But all formulas provide a foundational truth to an answer we seek. The formula I was looking for? The way to reach a foundational truth:

"How to be a great dad."

My subjects? A few dads whose leadership and dad-like abilities I've experienced first-hand. I saw their results (their children). I was impressed with their children. Therefore, I was impressed with their dad-abilities.

This formula contains some personal accounts of what would later become some of the most important experiences of my life, even though I didn't know it at the time. I didn't realize these events would shape me the way they did. Only later did I discover that what I'd been through actually instilled me with some fundamental beliefs and attributes that contribute to being a great dad.

Thanks to my observations of those men close to me— observations of their characteristics, attributes and behaviors, I realize now that those experiences created some crucial components of being a great dad. I didn't know it at the time, but I know it now.

And let's not forget, you instantly join the Dad Life Club the moment your first-born son or daughter enters this earth. But what does it take to live a Dad Life that has the most positive, long-lasting impact possible? I've got an idea.

Let me show you.

Let's discuss my *Dad Life Formula.*

First, a Solid Foundation

Our foundations are just that. The thing upon which we're built. You can have a strong foundation or a weak foundation. When a foundation is weak, everything you build on top of it is precarious at best, and usually comes crumbling down sooner rather than later. With a strong foundation, everything built on top of it holds equal strength and is less likely to crumble with time. It stands up to storms and keeps its contents safe and sound.

Everything comes back to the foundation. Our whole lives are built upon their foundation. We can and should, if we want answers, trace our lives back to their foundation.

While this book is not intended to be a book about what I believe outside of being a dad, I would be remiss if I didn't define my version of The Dad Life by talking about how I established my own foundation. My core. What makes me, well, me. What makes me such a passionate believer in my children.

Again, the best way to tell it, is through a story.

I was in the seventh grade. I remember being on a bus (here goes...another bus story). But this time, this bus had nothing to do with school. Our destination was nowhere near the front doors of my middle school. But the bus did hold about twenty students. And we were excited to get where we were going—a youth retreat

The twenty students with me were all students who attended my church. We were friends. All of us. We got along great. We created memories together over the years. Every year those memories got a little better and more solid and unforgettable. These retreats were a highlight in our young lives.

We picked a cool destination every year. Typically, they involved a bunch of cabins and a main congregation room. Our youth group band would lead our youth group in song— praise and worship songs. Afterwards, our youth pastor would share a short message from the Bible. His messages spoke of hope, and peace, and joy, and painted a picture for a positive road map for the future—all of them based on how Jesus impacts our lives.

I was always there. But I didn't always pay attention.

Each trip—and I attended them year after year—involved a pretty common intention and theme—to impact our lives based on teachings of the Bible and encourage us to live a life beyond reproach. A life in which we rose above the negative influences young people always meet and can easily fall victim to while growing up. To live a Christ-like life as best we could.
I remember a particular year that stands out from the rest, so much so that I even remember our cabin in near-photographic memory. I remember its rectangular shape, its light grey walls and worn carpet—so worn that we had to wear shoes if we wanted to walk around with any semblance of comfort.

I shared the cabin with about twelve guys around my age and a few who were a little older. We stayed up late enjoying funny conversations and just having a great time in general.

I remember our basketball games. That year, I considered myself a much better player than I actually was. And I remember meeting in the food hall. The food was great—and since I love food soooo much, the eating part was a major highlight, of course. And sharing it with the others every day is a particularly fond memory of that time.

Even though I recall those details so clearly, and even though those memories are special, they're not why I remember that trip more than the others.

It's because of this:

On the last night of our visit, we met in a tiny chapel. It was the same chapel we'd been visiting each night over the last several days of our time there.

But this night was different, a crystal clear memory—clearer than the rest. I don't think I'll ever forget that night as long as I live.

I sat on the right side of the room in the second row on the second chair to the left on one of the chapel's very dark green chairs. That's right, I remember the specific chair. Though a natural leader, my "follower" tendencies sometimes crept in— which was why I sat where I did—for the simple reason that my friends in the same row.

I sang the songs when the band was playing. I listened to the message when our youth pastor started speaking. But this time I was listening more intently than usual.

His message was simple: He spoke about living a life that

mattered. Living a life with God as my cornerstone.

I remember thinking about the word "cornerstone" and what it meant.

See, in the construction world, the cornerstone is a foundation stone. Its placement sets the basis for the placement of where all of the other stones will be laid. It's referenced. And it matters. The cornerstone helps set the position for a building's entire structure. *The entire structure.*

In the spiritual world, having God as my cornerstone means I would follow Him and His principles with every step I made in life. With each choice. He would be referenced. He would matter. He would help set my position, or my structure, for the rest of the moves in my life.

I heard this. I thought about this. And while I'd heard similar messages year after year, I remember thinking for the first time, yes! I want that! I need that!

His message continued. If we want God as our cornerstone, all we have to do is accept him as our Lord and Savior.

Even though I grew up in the church, it didn't mean that I was listening all that much. I mean really *listening* to what was preached each week.

But thankfully for me, that night, this youth pastor explained to me just how we can accept Him into our lives and make Him our cornerstone. Just make a simple prayer. So I did:

Dear Jesus,

Please come and live in my heart. Forgive me of my sins. Thank you for dying to take away my sins—all sins in the past, present, and future. I want to live according to your purpose. I love you.

Amen

I prayed this prayer. I accepted Jesus into my heart. I didn't fully understand what this meant at the time but I remember being told what it meant—that from now on my focus was to use God's principles as my cornerstone in life. I wanted a cornerstone and needed a foundation to go forward in life. I knew that I needed this and I made the commitment.

I've been living with God as my cornerstone ever since.

I Saw Things Differently

After I came home from my youth trip, after saying this prayer and committing to having God as my cornerstone, I started to notice things around me I wasn't looking for before.

I looked at the people I mentioned before (my dad, my brother, uncle, grandfather, and pastor). I realized they all had their own cornerstone of strength as well as a moral compass to guide their decisions. It helped them with the tough choices in life. It made them better leaders. Better decision-makers. And, from my perspective, much better dads.

I didn't know it at the time, but finding my cornerstone gave me a reference point for all the decisions to come. When I became a dad, and started to face dad challenges with my children, I had that foundation. It guided my questions, my choices, and my decisions. How should I lead them? How should I provide discipline to them? How would I guide them?

I knew where my answers would come from. From the teachings in the Bible—no matter the subject or emotion—it was all there for me in that Bible. From the words of God. It was that simple.

A solid foundation. *The first part of my formula.*

Second, Strong Support System

When I was in tenth grade, something unimaginable happened, something that would test me and my family—physically and emotionally for an entire year. It was the kind of thing I thought happened to other people. Then it happened to us.

I didn't see it coming, either. No one did.

I remember coming home from school. When I walked inside, my mom and dad were already there and I wasn't quite sure why. Dad worked a traditional job and didn't usually get home until after 5 o'clock.

But this day was a little different.

Not long after I walked through the doors, my mom said she

was going to run to the store.

I expected to hear my dad's usual joke.

"Can you take the car this time? Your feet will get tired!"

But this time he didn't say anything.

In a flurry of nervous motion, as she was leaving, mom looked at my dad and said, "carrots?"

"Sure…" he said.

"Bananas?"

"Yes."

"Apples?"

"All of them."

I still had my backpack on. I was a little confused. But it's funny the things you notice in times like these. It's funny what you remember. It wasn't normal for my dad to want fruit. He wasn't unhealthy, but fruits and veggies were never first in his line of snack preferences.

Then she was gone.

A few days later I was at my Thursday night youth group. Since my big brother had a car, I never needed a ride. But as we were leaving the upstairs part of the church, I saw my mom walk out of the church and hug one of her friends. She had tears in her eyes and she waved at me and my brother, saying, "I'll see you both at home."

I shrugged it off. Emotional situations weren't exactly my forte at that age.

When we got back to the house, my older brother and I found our parents sitting on the couch with my two younger sisters.

"We've got to talk," they said, as if they'd been waiting for us to get home.

And they had been waiting.

Now I really knew something was up.

Even though I was certainly sensitive, I didn't like to show my emotions—not to my friends, and especially not in front of my family.

Since I knew something was I up, I positioned myself on the edge of the couch, as far away from everyone as possible—and as close as possible to my own room in case I had to make a beeline outta there. It was my way of defending myself against what I knew was coming. Bad news.

My dad had cancer.

I wasn't really sure what that meant. I didn't know how it would impact our family or what was going to happen.

And just. like. that. my dad was in a hospital room in one of the top cancer facilities in the country. He had to be in there for a while for treatments. Then he'd be in a recovery center after that. The treatments and then the aftercare went on for months.

It felt like years.

But this story is NOT about my father's cancer. That full story would consume a book unto itself. This story is about something else. Something I slowly came to realize and notice more strongly with each passing day, week, and month of this very terrible year.

This story is about the overwhelming support system that grew up around my family right before my very eyes. All of a sudden, it seemed, family members and friends came in to fill in all the places that needed to be filled. They gave us strength when it felt like our whole world was falling down around us.

My dad was a great dad. A strong leader. A guy who could handle a situation when he needed to. One who had patience when it called for some. And one who laid the law down when I was acting out of line (which, I admit was way too frequently).

But at this time in his life, he was at a low point. He couldn't beat this on his own. He led a full life and kept a lot of things going.

But he couldn't do it all anymore. He needed help.

Help came.

My mom stepped into dad's shoes and became our family's leader. She was strong. For all of us. Me. My brothers and sisters. She had faith. Hope. Compassion. She stepped up in a big way. She hadn't had to lead the family before. My dad always did that. But when he was down and out, she stood strong and gave our family the confidence we needed to keep going.

My dad's whole family—his sisters, his brother-in law and sister-in law, his mom, dad, and in-laws—everyone was there, standing sentry, doing whatever needed doing, without us ever needing to ask. They devoted their time, their resources, and most importantly, their love to my dad, my mom, and our whole family. They built a perimeter of strength, love, and prayer around us when we were weak. They encircled us with protection and care and kept us going when we didn't think we could go on. Our family and friends were there when we needed them.

They supported us.

My dad's company and co-workers did everything they could to help, too. They assured then reassured my dad that his job was secure and would be there waiting for his return once he had healed. They provided a company car to my mom to travel to and from the hospital at no cost to our family. His paychecks still showed up regularly to keep us going. The company was there when we needed them.

They supported us.

In the midst of this family storm, this strong support system kept my father's family from falling apart. And while my dad was weak, he knew that his cornerstone (God) provided him and his family spiritual, emotional and physical strength in all kinds of ways. His cornerstone combined with our family support system was invaluable.

My dad got better. But it took time. Lots of time. It took patience. It took lots of doctor visits followed by follow-ups and more follow-ups. We cried. We prayed. But we did not lose hope.

My dad has recovered. He is back to the dad I remembered from before his long battle with cancer. And he's even stronger now. Because of his support system—friends, family, work, us. Even though he's a great dad, he couldn't have continued being a great dad without that support system.

Every dad goes through a low point in life. It may a low point as heavy and extreme as the cancer my father endured and beat, but we all go through challenging periods when nothing but a support system will get us through. Just knowing that we have that great support system—and then experiencing that support system working when it's most needed—gives us the ultimate assist when it comes to remaining a great dad.

Watching how our family was cared for during my dad's cancer—and seeing all the support that sprung up around him and his family, I realized that a dad is only as great as the support system that surrounds him.

Just as a king ruling his land is only as strong as the walls that surround it, a dad is only as strong as the perimeter he has around his own castle. I knew that my greatness as a dad needed that same solid—and I mean rock-solid— support system.

A support system. *An invaluable part of the Dad Life equation.*

Lastly, Tough Love

I came out of my bedroom with a smile on my face and a game plan in my head. I was pretty excited to tell my dad about it. I tended to consider myself a genius. Even when it came to the simple things. Like this awesome plan.

"Hey Dad," I said in an overconfident voice, a slight smirk spreading across myself. The smirk was uncontrollable. A direct reflexive result of the thrilling plan I couldn't wait to share with my dad.

I told him about the extra $400 I'd saved up. I knew just what I was going to use it for, too. It was something I deserved. A wise choice, in my opinion.

My planned purchase?

Well, that would be a shiny new deluxe stereo system. I even had the perfect spot for it in my bedroom where the acoustics would just shine. I'd sit in my room listening to the best music bouncing into my ears with crystal-clear perfection.

I did my research. I knew what I wanted. I selected the spot where it would go. And best of all, I had the money to buy it. I had the money to buy every bit of that stereo. On my own. Just like my dad taught me.

Or so I thought.

As I began to tell him my plan, his facial response didn't match the one I'd thought I would see. I knew he had a response coming. And I could tell that it wasn't quite the one I was looking for.

The one of approval.

"I think it's a great idea that you get your stereo," he said to me.

"Really?"

I responded with hesitancy because I knew something more was coming.

I was 17. And had learned a lot of life lessons from my dad. And I'd followed through with them. I had my own cell phone bill that I paid promptly each month. I also had my own Camaro. That's right, this thing was a beautiful hunter green with shiny rims and thick cloth interior—all of which I maintained to perfection. Me. No one else detailed that car. To top it off, I was a great kid who had excellent grades.

So what gave?

"You can get the stereo after your car is paid off."

His tone was calm, even relaxing. But it was serious. I didn't quite get it. Here I was. I had the $400 I needed for the stereo. I had about $800 left to pay off my car. While I paid for most of it, my parents had helped me get it. So the "loan" I'd received was a loan from my parents. The money I owed on the car. I owed it to the bank operated by my dad. Which, in this case, was his wallet.

I pleaded with him to give me the logic behind his request. I wasn't going to stop the payments. I didn't understand.

He helped me out with that. He told me that I should take care of my first responsibilities, well, first. Honor your commitments. Get ahead if you can. But never settle for the bare minimum. If your payment is $100 a month, pay $200 when you can. You'll settle your debt more quickly. Then you'll have the joy of freedom and flexibility once the debt is settled.

This didn't make sense to me then. Not for a long time. But it made sense to me eventually—and that was when I became a dad myself.

What he was doing in this moment is what I call tough love. He took the opportunity to give me a life lesson even though he knew I'd be disappointed. He knew I'd eventually learn. And he didn't budge on his stance just because I gave him pushback.

He knew that my pushback may have left him unsettled in the moment, but it would teach me something in the future.

It was tough for both of us.

He was willing to go through all that so I would have a better life and be a better person.

But at the time, it made zero sense to me. He could have let me buy that stereo that I wanted. I could have listened to great music on a great stereo, but the stereo would have eventually run through its life-force and died like all electronics do. His lesson left me with a much better reward than I could have imagined at the time.

Months later, after I paid off my car, he asked me when I was going to buy that stereo. I didn't owe any debts and my bank account had some extra money but I didn't want the stereo anymore. I decided to save it instead of waste it. Another lesson.

Go figure.

This kind of teaching, one when you're willing to go the extra mile to give a good lesson while knowingly disappointing your child, is a necessary skill for dads. These lessons may cause your child to push back and get mad at you. But, you're willing—as a dad—to take the brunt of it and not give in, because you know your children will learn an invaluable life lesson that will make the rest of their lives better. Tough love matters. It matters a lot. Use it whenever and however you can.

Tough Love. *Taking one for the team to give your child a better* *future.*

The Dad Life Formula

It's a simple concept. One that can be easily established, carried out throughout your entire life as a dad, and provide a lasting and impactful relationship with your children.

Be a Dad

+

Have a Solid Foundation

+

Create a Strong Support System

+

Deploy Tough Love

=

The Dad Life

Follow these simple steps and I know that it will improve your Dad Life, your children's lives, and your whole life.

Onward, Dads

As we continue our journey as dads—taking into account some of the tools, tricks, and focal points of this book—there's one thing you must never forget. If you forget this, you'll sell yourself short.

You are not perfect. You will mess up. You will make mistakes. You will feel defeated at times. You will feel like you didn't make the right choices sometimes.

Ultimately, there are no official rules to being a dad. Focus on being the best dad you can be. Focus your attention on the kinds of people you want your children to be—good people with confidence and strong values. Love them to death. Hug them. Kiss them. And then hug and kiss them some more. Cherish every moment. Put them first. Don't wait until the end of your life to realize that to love and to be loved is the most important thing in the world. And your children will be grown in the blink of the eye. You can't take missed moments back. So grab onto them now. Life is fleeting.

You have one precious life. So do your children. You have one chance at being a dad.

Make it count.

#DadLife

Thanks, Everyone

Wow, what a journey! This book experience has been incredible. Amazing. I took a long trip down memory lane and didn't want to come back. At all. But, here I am.

And before I completely call this book a wrap, there are some people in my life that I would love to thank. Let's get sentimental. Only for a moment. After all, without them, this book would have never come to fruition. Or maybe it would have. But it probably would have been pretty boring.

First, I must thank my Heavenly Father, who provides me with the strong foundation I need to lead my life and my family in the manner that best serves the world with a true definition of love (1 Corinthians 13:4-8) that I can pass along to my children and for helping me to always be faithful no matter what happens. You are everything to me!

Next, the most important person in my life, Jewel. My wife, yes. But more importantly, my best friend. The one who is there no matter what. And I mean, no matter what. She's heard these stories and through it all, she is still there for me. I know, pretty impressive, right? I love you!

Jamison, my son, blesses me with the privilege of non-stop entertainment. The list of words with which to describe this child are almost endless. Funny. Witty. Charming. Handsome. I don't have enough room here to explain his personality with the completeness I'd like. But in short, he is amazing. His title—my son—is one I'm rather proud of.

My "little" joy in life is my daughter, Victoria. She's spent time writing in her journal while I've written this book on many occasions—just so we had time to do something we both loved, together. Her kindness overflows to everyone around her. She's contagious. You'd love it. And you'd love her. Just as I do.

Kaila is my stepdaughter by definition, but my daughter by heart. I'm blessed she has joined our family. Without her, I wouldn't have anyone to help enforce the rules in our home. Because, trust me, she's great at helping me!

To all three of my children, I can't wait for you to be able to read and understand just what everything in this book is about. One day you will, and you'll know just how passionate and excited I am to be your dad and to lead you the best way I know how! And for you to know how funny you are. And how great you are. And how much I love you. No matter what!

Where did I get a ton of my influence from? My dad of course. I would introduce him to you as Charlie. But to me, he's dad. And he's a great one. After all, he endured the trials of raising a child like me! And he did it with grace, strength, wisdom and abundant patience. But look how I turned out! Not bad. And he's a huge reason why. So, thanks, dad!

My caring side? Well, my mom, Vicky, gets all the credit there. Do you need something? Yep, she's there! Do you need help? Of course, she'll help. Need someone who will listen to you? Not even a second goes by before she'll say "of course!" She's taught me how to do the same thing. My mom has more amazing qualities than I can put into words here. In short, I'm so lucky to have had such a positive influence in my life. As a child and as a "grown-up."

Thank you to my brother Aaron, who let me tag along all those years he was in high school even though I was that "pesky younger brother." You taught me how to lead my oldest son to be a great older brother.

Thank you to my sister Rachel, who has forgiven me for all those miserable years I gave her (and there were many of them). You taught me about forgiveness.

Thank you to my youngest sister Ashley, for being so special, the one sibling who's always wanted to take a different path in life. You've taught me to think differently and to think outside of the box. Always.

Oh yeah, there are many many many more people who've had influence on me, which ultimately influenced this book.

My grandfather, who I call "Gido," who always took the time to teach me a life lesson. My grandfather Charles who was always direct and taught me the way things should be. My grandmother Grace who taught me to double check my spelling and to formulate a well-thought-out sentence and always knew how make someone feel special. And my grandma Carol, who taught me that my faith should lead me in all areas of my life.

To the person who endured countless hours editing this book, Ama. She is insanely talented with a pen. Well, in our case, a keyboard. She helped motivate and challenge me to become a more creative writer. Thank you!

The finer details are important as well, right? Without Anna, this book may have typos and extra spaces and mispelingz (just kidding). She is great. And thorough.

To my pastors, best friend, brothers in Christ, aunts, uncles, cousins and random people in grocery stores I've seen treat their children with respect and kindness, thank you. Thank you for every lesson you've taught me. Because every lesson helps shape someone. And in this case, that person was me.

And thank you, to everyone with this book in your hands. I hope it gives you some laughs and hopefully inspires you and lets you in on some tips to help you be the best dad you can be.

Thanks, everyone.

About the Author

Hey, there's this guy who just wrote his first book. His name is Chris Bultman and he lives in Jacksonville, Florida, with his stunning wife, three beautiful children, and a tiny dog. He loves Jesus, playing sports, sushi, reading about Abraham Lincoln, and is super active and dedicated to his church and his community and owes his good life to God and his steadfast faith.

Chris also owns his own marketing company, is always busy, and is insanely creative and analytical at the same time. He's also one of the nicest guys you'll ever meet. Chris is a fiend for coffee and eighties movies and just has amazing taste in general.

So this book is about his family. Especially about raising his family—his children. It's about his life as a dad and a son and a person in this world and especially what he's experienced and learned in his Dad Life. During the course of writing this book, he's come up with a few more ideas for more books. So, look forward to further awesomeness from this new writer. Oh, and he's really Rambo in disguise.